T0329196

THE LIFE AND JOURNEY OF AN ENTREPRENEUR

THE LIFE AND JOURNEY OF AN ENTREPRENEUR

Katongo Mulenga Maine

Gadsden Publishers

Gadsden Publishers
P.O. Box 32581, Lusaka, Zambia

ISBN 978 9982 24 1090

INTRODUCTION

Katongo Maine's is the first book to be published in a new series of memoirs, entitled *Remarkable Women of Zambia*, that will show how women in this country have made their mark in politics, civil society, education, business and NGOs. Women were always involved in Zambia's Independence struggle and after it was achieved they queued alongside men to vote in the first elections. They have never given up their involvement in public life but, as elsewhere, it was men who slipped into most positions of real power and stayed there. For women throughout the world, the struggle to fulfil their potential continues and it is hoped that this series will not only claim a place for the remarkable women who figure in Zambia's modern history but also act as an inspiration to younger women today.

The series is initially founded on the work of the *Chipembi Alumni Writers' Group* which meets informally to encourage its members in the difficult task of creating both memoir and fiction – there just isn't enough literature produced in Zambia and the *Chipembi Alumni* are determined to remedy that, but it is hoped that other new authors with different backgrounds will come forward with their own life-stories.

In colonial Northern Rhodesia education was racially segregated, there were few opportunities for formal secondary education for African children – and if it was bad for boys it was even worse for girls. Established not by the Northern Rhodesian Government but by the Methodist Church, *Chipembi* was the only school in the whole country to provide African girls with the full secondary education that could take them on to university and the professions. Competition for admission was fierce, so *Chipembi* girls were acknowledged to be an intellectual elite. They were truly modern women and were pretty formiddable. It was inevitable that the school's alumni would constitute the first generation of prominent women in independent Zambia and that old school friendships would become the basis of a network of support for this newly emerging category. It was equally inevitable that *Chipembi* alumni would marry some of Zambia's most successful men.

Katongo Maine's story tells of a remarkable young girl from a poor family who defied her mother by refusing an arranged marriage, determined instead to become a nurse with a career and salary of her own. Against all the odds, she gained a place at *Chipembi* through her own hard work, but when she arrived there found that it was a real shock. She writes about the way the school taught self reliance, bringing her into contact with new ideas and, importantly, with women teachers who were self-supporting spinsters.

At school her horizons widened and, whilst still a teenager, Katongo was offered a place to study nursing in East Germany, a country she knew absolutely nothing about, where she would have to learn a new language before commencing her training. Katongo recounts her experience of the strange ways of her hosts, their peculiar food, the cold and the clothes that went with it. She didn't realise it at the time but, with Independence looming in African states, both the Communist Bloc and the West were competing to train the new professionals who would replace the colonial administrators and businessmen and Katongo was a part of this process. She left colonial Northern Rhodesia with all the social and career restrictions involved and returned as a qualified nursing sister to independent Zambia with a new view of the world and her place in it, but if her German sponsors thought she would be an agent of African socialism they'd miscalculated.

Throughout her memoir, Katongo's determination to be successful shines through and her abiding goal was to be very wealthy in her own right. Eventually nursing was unable to satisfy her boundless ambition and we find her retraining as a dress designer in New York when she joined her husband who was studying at the University of Columbia. To finance her own course and to supplement her husband's tiny grant, Katongo worked at night as a nurse – attending college in the day and juggling her role as a mother, there was little time for pleasure or a social life and she is disparaging of the diplomatic wives who treated their time in New York as a free holiday. On her return to Zambia we see her designing for a new cosmopolitan market, setting up a dress factory, specialising in wedding gowns and establishing the most prestigious dress shop in Lusaka. Constantly expanding and investing, she moved into import/export, becoming a millionaire in her own right. She was never afraid to undertake work that others thought demeaning or daunting if that was the best way to raise essential capital; so we find her getting up early to drive to Kafue to buy fresh fish for the Lusaka market or making the long trip up to the Northern Province alone to source *kapenta* and caterpillars. The range of her trading exploits is staggering – one of her biggest coups was to arrange to fly fresh beef from Zambia to Mozambique.

But Katongo was not just a successful businesswoman. She is a daughter, sister, wife and mother and she invites her readers into the intimacies of her family life with her journalist husband and her two much-loved sons. Readers become party to decisions about the boys' education, sending them to school abroad. She tells us about the move to a farm outside Lusaka that becomes the focus of many parties. She also reveals her own spiritual unease and her eventual conversion to Christian Science.

On top of everything else, Katongo was drawn into political life. Disillusioned with the policies of the One Party State, particularly matters regarding business enterprise, she became a founder member of the Movement for Multiparty Democracy and was returned as an MP in the 1991 election. In acknowledgement of her hard-fought campaign she was appointed as a junior minister, but found relations with President Chiluba difficult (to say the least). Politics was not her natural home and things started to fall apart with political skullduggery and a series of investment setbacks. She hit her all-time low in 2002, falling into a severe depression when her husband and son died in the same year. Katongo does not hold back or gloss over her personal grief and the way her business empire fell apart. There is much to be learned from her account of this bleak time and how she came out of it.

People who write their autobiographies are brave – they offer their lives up for others to scrutinise and they know that there will inevitably be criticism (sometimes vicious) and gossip. A memoirist would have to be a saint not to try to put herself in the best possible light and critics often accuse them of vanity, but this is unfair. From accounts like Katongo's readers can learn about the times the writers lived through – dry history comes alive as one follows the fate of someone one comes to know and care about. Unlike academic history, memoir is unabashed about being written from a single point of view and there is no denying that Katongo's story is that of a particularly determined and talented woman, but she is also a woman who experiences the same doubts and set-backs as the rest of us.

Now in her seventies and retired from much of her business activity, Katongo looks back in this fascinating book on her full life, she tells us how she now takes pleasure in her status as a grandmother, but she is no ordinary "Granny" – she is also busily involved in reafforestation in Muchinga Province! I am proud to have been asked to edit this series and I am eagerly awaiting the next life-history of another remarkable Zambian woman.

Pamela Shurmer-Smith

PREFACE

Child Marriage

More than anything else, I want to share my experiences with the girls out there and urge them that they should fight this scourge tooth and nail; after all it is their lives at stake.

The issue of child marriage has been with us as long as we can remember, and the sad thing is, the reasons for this cruel and destructive action remain the same. Namely: poverty and ignorance. Due to poverty parents blindly consider their daughter a one-off merchandise that will solve the bad situation they find themselves in. Unfortunately 99.9% of the time they do not realize how few and short lived the benefits are. The only thing that is 100% sure is the fact that the girl's life is irreparably ruined. And yet if that girl had an education the parents would comfortably be taken care of for the rest of their lives, because she would turn out to be their steady passive income. Therefore, there is a glorious life for the girl child harnessed within the confines of classroom walls.

In the African family set-up, educated daughters have proved to be more caring and responsible towards their parents' welfare, as well as the family. However, the vicious circle of child-marriage will end only when the society and parents at large begin considering the girl child as the goose that lays the golden egg and not one-off merchandise.

I am a living example of the goose that could have been a one-off merchandise. Had my parents succeeded in marrying me off at the age of fifteen I would never have become: a nurse, a fashion designer, a successful CEO of my own enterprises, a world-travelled person, a Member of Parliament, and a Minister in the government of my country, Zambia.

I pray and trust this book will fall into the hands of the girl child before she becomes that 'one-off merchandise'. Rick Warren said in his book *The Purpose Driven Life:* "The things you're most embarrassed about, most ashamed of, and most reluctant to share are the tools God can use most powerfully to heal others."

I have been criticized for being too frank. Unfortunately this happens to be my nature which I cannot run away from. I felt this book should not be one of those that begins and ends with success stories only. To give an objective and balanced account there have to be some good and bad events in any life story. Having written about many people in this book, I have attempted to be as factual as I possibly can be, because I am aware that people will always pass judgement on the contents as they read.Some people may disagree with certain views, but this is a story of my life, its challenges, disappointments, shortcomings and many a time God's favors.

Writing about oneself is not easy because there is always a possibility to overstate or understate one's virtues.

This edition has been prompted by the fact that CHILD MARRIAGE LEVELS have gotten out of hand. I felt I had a rich story to tell to the young generation that this deadly scourge can be challenged HEAD ON!!

PART ONE

My Early Days

A Fateful Day

Sometimes an ordinary day dawns, but by nightfall one's life has been turned upside down. There was a day like that in 1958, when I was just fifteen years old and living in Lusaka. I was on holiday from school, staying with Dorothy, my elder sister, and I remember it as if it were yesterday. She rested a hand on my shoulder and said softly, "There is something I have to say to you and I am sure it will really upset you. Are, you ready to hear it?"

With no inkling what was in store for me, I nodded apprehensively.

"They have found you a man to marry; you will not be going back to school."

I was paralyzed, speechless and confused. I loved school and had ambitions. I wanted to train as a nurse. I wanted a career. I wanted, above everything, to be independent and take command of my own life. My parents were shattering my dream without even consulting me.

My mother had sent Beatrice, my ten years' younger sister, as the messenger to deliver her threat that, 'if Selina does not come straight to me of her own accord, I will come there, beat her and drag her to the man who wants to marry her.'

My mother and I had never been able to get on and, to avoid her invective, I preferred to spend my school holidays with Dorothy and her husband, Ephraim. I enjoyed their company and derived peace of mind in their home, where there was so much harmony.

"OK let's go to her then!" I muttered through gritted teeth.

Beatrice and I strode in silence to our family home, my heart bleeding and full of anger. I felt confused and rejected and on arrival there I confronted my mother, sobbing, and I poured out my heart to the woman who should have loved me.

"Mother, I know you hate me for reasons only known to yourself, but I did not know that your hatred was this strong. How could you deliberately thwart my ambitions and destroy my life?" I hoped she might understand the depth of my misery for once, but no.

"Beatrice, just take her to the man who wants to marry her," she yelled.

Docilely, I followed Beatrice through the township to a strange man's house – I was like a sheep being led to the slaughter. We found my prospective 'husband' sitting outside on a stool. When he saw us he stood up and bade us enter his one-roomed home. I cast my eyes quickly over the stranger and could not see what had attracted my mother. I wondered whether she was so blinded with loathing that she could only wish me ill and did not care what happened to me. Or perhaps he'd given her something? My mind was racing, but I certainly was having nothing to do with this appalling marriage prospect. His shirt collar was torn, his jacket was patched at the elbows, trousers patched on the knees, and the brown unpolished shoes that had seen many rainy seasons had been mended on the toes.

"Whoa! Oh God help, me!" I prayed silently.

Somehow it was good that he was not expecting us. Had he known of our coming he probably would have dressed better, but his appearance justified my stand, and made me angrier and more determined to have absolutely nothing to do with this arrangement. Even if I had wanted to marry, this was certainly not my dream husband.

Tears welled up in my eyes again, but I held them back. I noticed the man seemed uncomfortable even in his own domain. He must have read my mood and body language, displaying the uncompromising contempt only a teenaged girl is capable of. After a long silence he cleared his throat and shiftily uttered, "I was thinking, I was thinking, I was thinking," nervously repeating himself several times, "that if God willing we can marry".

Almost hysterically I yelled, "Marry who? Which God, and I mean *which* God would allow such a mismatch? You are not educated, and I am educated, NO! NO! No God would allow such. From the outset there is no compatibility between us, my mere speaking of English will be a bone of contention and a reason for quarrelling, even beating me up. My sincere advice is for you to go and marry one of your fellow illiterates. By the way, have you ever even set eyes on me before?"

As I look back I realise how cruel my words were, but I was horrified as I contemplated the future that he and my mother had determined for me.

"No, I have never seen you," he answered, his eyes cast down abjectly.

"So how could you just accept there is a 'Selina' and you'd be happy to marry her? What kind of a man are you who cannot find a wife on his own, what if this Selina had one leg, or happened to be loony?"

I was indeed livid – incensed with this man but even more with my parents, who had landed me in this mess. I stormed out of his house, indifferent to the offence I was causing, my little sister tagging behind, bewildered by what she had witnessed.

Back with my mother, I told her that I had given the stranger a piece of my mind. She looked up to heaven as if in prayer and chillingly said, "I curse you and I curse you that you will have no good luck in your life, and no man will ever want to marry you because you have refused the man of our choice."

Surprising myself with my boldness, I assured my mother that whatever she said just went in through my left ear and flew out through the right, because even the Almighty God knew that I had done nothing to warrant her curse. Seeing that I was adamant, she turned her anger on my father who was silently busy at his carpenter's bench; she accused him of weakness for not disciplining me and not acting like a real man.

I'd always been closer to Daddy and he retorted, "Haah! Don't drag me into your madness. You created this for yourself. I told you from the beginning to leave the poor girl alone to continue with school, but you do not want to see sense – the girl has always been the top of her class but you want to ruin her future with your mad plans."

I realized that this was actually Mother's scheme alone but also that she was determined to succeed. Feeling wretched, I sat down on the veranda and cried. I concluded I had reached a dead end and there seemed to be no obvious way out of this appalling marriage arrangement. Then I resolved that over my dead body would I allow that to happen. I promised myself that I might be just fifteen years old but, one way or another, I was determined to continue my education.

When I was young, children had no right to question their parents' decision when it concerned marriage. Girls, especially, did as they were told, but that morning I was convinced that that was neither fair, nor right. The world was changing and a good education was my dream. I was sure that I was being guided at every stage by the Almighty God and this gave me the strength to defy my parents and convention. Within the community I could see that people who were comparatively well-off, such as Mr Safeli Chileshe (the man who was to become the first black Mayor of Lusaka) sent their daughters to school, rather than marrying them off at a tender age. I wanted the same chances as those daughters of the elite. Several of my schoolmates had married young and put up no resistance – they were even proud to become wives and mothers, but that course was not for me.

I was still crying on the verandah when our eldest brother, Lebby, came to visit and my heart leaped with joy, assuming that he would be my saviour. Our brother was not just Mother's first born, but also the apple of her eye and I hoped he would coax her into seeing sense about my future. On seeing me he immediately asked, "What is the matter, why is she crying?"

Mother answered, "We found her a man to marry her, but she does not want to follow our wishes."

I was stunned when he turned to face me with a sneer and said, "What's the big deal? Why the fuss? Women are here to marry and bear children. Hey, just get married!"

Lebby's comments pierced my heart like a double-edged sword. I had thought that, as a modern young man, he would be sympathetic, but no, here he was, rubbing salt into an

5

open wound. I pulled myself together, stood up, wiping the tears with the back of both my hands, and said to myself, 'Selina you are on your own, girl.'

Defiantly I confronted my brother, "Lebby, let me tell you something now. I am going to show you just how wrong you are. I'll prove to you that a woman can do many things and achieve a lot, contrary to your stupid beliefs about just being good for marrying and having children."

I felt angry, bitter, helpless and rejected by the very people who should have supported me. I began to walk back to Dorothy's house and quietly started talking to God: "God where are you when all this wickedness from my family is happening? What do you want me to do? I do not want to marry yet, I want to train as a nurse. God, remember, I have always cried to you, that you are both my heavenly and earthly mother because this mother here does not love me. I believe she is not even my real mother."

I mourned as if I were an orphan. Along the way there was a huge old fig tree where I sat down and, leaning against its rough trunk, cried my heart out. The weather was chilly although it was August, the beginning of the hot season. I don't know how long I sat there sobbing; I only realized that I had cried myself out when it was dusk. I got up knowing that my life had irrevocably turned a corner – I wondered what would lie ahead, but I was determined that, whatever it was, it was not going to be ordinary.

Family and Childhood

You have to believe in yourself when no one else does, that is what makes you a winner.

Venus Williams, Tennis Champion

I was born in 1943 in Mukosela village, in the Northern Province of what was at that time still colonial Northern Rhodesia. In my family we were eight children, five girls and three boys. Lebby was the first born, followed by Dorothy, I was the third born child, then came another girl, Raphy, two boys, Joseph, and Lloyd and finally two more girls, Beatrice and Musakanya.

Dad was a softly spoken person who expressed parental love to all his children. His disciplinary measures were fair if need arose. Unlike many of our neighbours, Mum and Dad never fought and quarrelled in our presence, so I grew up believing it was a perfect home despite the poverty that engulfed the family. But whereas Mother loved, lavished and idolized her male children to the point of spoiling them, convinced that they were never wrong, we girls were often spanked, reprimanded and called all sorts of names. Of all my siblings, I am the smallest in stature but I have turned out to be the pillar of the family. This reminds me of what my English friend, Annie Fraenkel, once said about being small. When she was a little girl she complained to her mother that schoolmates were bullying and teasing her and her mum's answer was, "Don't worry my dear, precious gifts come in small parcels, not large packages."

Over the years I have become convinced that I am that precious gift in a small parcel to my family.

Growing up in Southern and Northern Rhodesia

I am told we left the village with Mum and Dorothy, my sister, when I was three years old to join Dad, who was working in Bulawayo in Southern Rhodesia where we lived in Mzilikazi Location. Dad's first employment had been at Bwana Mukubwa mine in Ndola and I guess that is where he learnt his carpentry trade before he went to Bulawayo. We returned to NR when I was ten years old and settled in Lusaka. Though this was prior to the establishment of the Central African Federation, Northern Rhodesians often travelled to Southern Rhodesia seeking employment. Unbelievably some men walked all the way to Wankie and

Kamativi mines, as well as places such as Bulawayo, if they could not afford the train fare. Yes, sure there was also paid work in the cities of Northern Rhodesia, otherwise people would not have left their villages in search of jobs.

When I turned seven, Dorothy and I were both enrolled in Sub A at Lobengula School in Bulawayo, though she was older than I. The beginning was tough because of the unprecedented discrimination and bullying from schoolmates who called us 'AMAZAMBEZI', but in Sub-B I developed some courage and I fought back if anyone attacked me or my sister. There was a girl called Selina who persistently picked a quarrel with me over our shared name. One day I just decided enough was enough and I said, "You know what? Where we come from when we fight we aim to kill, so just try me!"

When she charged at me I punched her on the nose and blood spattered as she staggered and fell heavily to the ground. All her supporters scampered as I was inviting anyone to dare me, boys and girls. From then on she and her supporters left my sister and me in peace and I'd learned a valuable lesson about standing up for myself.

Returning to (then) Northern Rhodesia

When I was ten years old and the family came back to Northern Rhodesia, we settled in Lusaka. At that time the only residential compounds for the indigenous people were Kabwata and Chinika; both having round, grass-thatched one-roomed houses. Then the colonial masters of the day built Chilenje Suburb which was predominantly for civil servants; houses here were decent, two- and three-roomed, with a corrugated iron roof, outside toilet and communal water tap. My family settled in Chinika Compound and I enrolled at Chinika Primary School.

Matero Suburb was under construction at the time and its houses resembled those of Chilenje so we moved there as soon as it was finished, though we continued commuting to Chinika School until the end of that academic year, before transferring to Mulongoti School.

At Chinika School in Standard 3 the class teacher introduced the 'Queen and King of the Class' competition. Every Friday he would announce the week's results and put the names of the highest scoring girl and boy on the board. I used to score the highest for the whole class and was named 'Queen of the Class' all the time, but the King's slot used to go to Jeremiah Ngoma, Gilbert Chileshe, Stewart Mhango or Albert Mumba. The five of us were the youngest and yet we were the cream of the class. The bullies were much older and really made our lives miserable during break time. At the end of each term the Headmaster would announce the overall results and when he called "Standard 3, Selina Mulenga" I would burst into tears out of fear of being hammered. As a grown woman, married with two children, I ran into Roy (Albert) Mumba, my old classmate, who was by then the Chief Executive Officer for Lever Brothers Zambia Limited. He told me he'd always wondered why I cried each time my name was called as Number One, when for him it was reason for jubilation.

"Were those tears of joy?"

"No Roy, those were tears of fear. Do you remember Ruth, the great bully in our class?"

It is strange how we can remember being tormented so long ago, even when we realise that our tormentors were people who can never succeed, but disappear without trace into mundane lives – but as the British say, 'What doesn't kill you makes you stronger.' During my primary school days, from Standard 4 to 5, in 1954-56, my family experienced a lot of financial hardship, to the point of my having to wear just the one school uniform for close to three years. This was during the years just before Roy Welensky became the Prime Minister of the Federation of Rhodesia and Nyasaland, and the white supremacist agenda of Federation prompted more people in Northern Rhodesia to join in the struggle for Independence. Northern Rhodesians were already very politically active; there was a lot of industrial unrest particularly by the workers in the mines. The Bemba people were in the forefront as union and political activists; this made them a clear target whenever colonial employers decided on punitive measures in reaction to strikes and agitation.

Although they continued to be the dominant group among mineworkers, increasingly it became difficult for Bemba men to find jobs. Many European employers would ask for chitupa (ID-identity card), and once it was established that a person was a Bemba, an existing vacancy would suddenly become unavailable. It was said that the Bembas were viewed as argumentative and stubborn so were denied jobs especially on the line of rail, even as far south as Southern Rhodesia. A classic example was narrated to me by Mr Kaluba:

"A colonial farmer once gave a contract to a builder bearing a Nyanja name on his ID, but when the building part was completed the roof was to be done by his partner. The white farmer on noticing a new person on the roof asked for his ID and, discovering that the carpenter bore a Bemba name, became furious and immediately cancelled the contract. The Bemba man was adamant and demanded that full payment be made for his work."

This prejudice against Bemba workers created untold suffering in the affected homes. My father was a carpenter by trade, he was a reserved person and not a trouble-maker at all, but by virtue of his being Bemba he was not exempt from this widespread discrimination; as a consequence he became self-employed, making tables, chairs, and beds.

Until our father became properly established, Dorothy's husband came to the rescue of the Mulenga family. For quite a while he unfailingly bought us a bag of maize meal every month and paid the rent for our house to the municipality. He himself was Bisa by tribe, so was not affected by the wrath of the white man on the Bemba. My brother-in-law worked for JW Jagger, a wholesale company, as a shop assistant; he did not earn much, but he shared the little he had, unlike Lebby,

10

our elder brother, who earned much more but never saw the plight of his own flesh and blood. My sister, Dorothy was not idle either, she made and sold fritters, and also made cushion covers for chairs to supplement the family income.

The entrepreneur in me

As a child I liked school, but also playing. During school holidays I spent most of my time with my friend, Foster Nauluta. She was pretty, quiet and well behaved. She was the first born of her parents. Her father was a builder by trade and her mother was a marketeer who sold dry beans, kapenta and groundnuts at Matero market in Lusaka. As soon as school broke up for the holidays, Foster's mother would leave the market business to Foster and stay at home. I was at the market daily helping my friend to sell her mother's merchandise. I enjoyed doing that and at the same time it gave me chance to be with my friend Foster whom I liked because she kept away from mischief, unlike many of my other age-mates. At the end of school holidays Foster's mother would give her some money to buy whatever she wanted, but I did not have that kind of luxury. However, after two holidays I had learnt about selling and found myself something I could trade in, to make some pocket money.

I started making munkoyo, a non-alcoholic drink, when I was just 12 years old. I would walk from Matero where we lived with a bucket of munkoyo on my head, and position myself at the Central Africa Road Services (CARS) bus stop on Great North Road and sell my merchandise there. I was so committed and enthusiastic about this business that I had to forgo playtime with my best friend. Initially my business days were Monday, Wednesday and Friday, because my starting capital was small. Subsequently, the days increased to Monday through to Friday. The business was good; I would always walk back home with an empty bucket and money in my pocket. At the end of each school holiday I was able to buy for myself a pair of shoes, underwear, and cloth to make a dress or two, but this income was not enough

11

to buy me a new school uniform as well. At this early age I was able to sew a simple dress for myself so my appearance improved, unlike my siblings, who continued to be in tatters; this encouraged me to continue selling during every school holiday thereafter.

Foster's tragedy was that she just could not make it in class. She was married off after she failed Standard 3, hopelessly, at the age of thirteen. Much later in life when I inquired about her I was told she had died in childbirth.

Even as a child, I would often brag to my friends that I would be a rich woman when I grew up. My friends would in turn taunt and laugh at me, "Look who is talking! Right now you happen to be the poorest amongst us, so just tell us where those riches will come from! Don't you think you are just a day dreamer, overtaken by wishful thinking?"

"I am not just going to be rich but I am going to have one or two children only," I would say.

At this stage I had convinced myself that all the poverty in my family was due to there being too many children. It was in this colonial context that my mother saw my early marriage as a way of alleviating family poverty – one less mouth to feed and no school expenses. But it was a short-sighted view.

My Plan B

A few days after the BOMBSHELL from my parents, I began thinking what I might do to take charge of my own life. I had successfully completed Form I at Chipembi Girls' Secondary School and wanted to go up into Form II, but that was expensive. If I couldn't continue in school, what was my 'plan B'? How could I resolve this problem that was so much bigger than I? I knew I could apply for nursing at Mukinge Mission Hospital with just my Standard Six Certificate and, though this would give me a lower qualification than I really wanted, it would be better than nothing, as long as I could become a career woman. I wrote my application and mailed it.

One warm September afternoon, I left Dorothy's house for a stroll and met one of our neighbours who greeted me with, "Hello Selina my dear, congratulations! I understand you have found a suitor. That is good, you will invite us for dinner one of these days."

He said this innocently, but I burst into hysterics. People turned to look, wondering if the man had assaulted me because I was screaming at the top of my voice. Initially he could not understand what he'd done to provoke this outburst, but eventually realised that I was crying because I did not want to be married. He came closer and embraced me until I stopped crying.

"I can see you don't think much of the prospect of becoming a wife."

"Absolutely, I want to go back to school, but I have no one to pay my fees."

There was silence and then he said, "Supposing I could find a bursary for you, how would you manage with transport to and from school as well as pocket money? Will your sister's husband, Ephraim, be willing to help?"

I was sure he would. This neighbour, Mr Luke Mwananshiku, and my brother-in-law had known each other for a long time. They belonged to the same congregation and occasionally he visited Ephraim at home, which is how I came to know him. He worked for the Immigration Department and was one of the few educated people that the British began employing in the Civil Service.

Early one morning Mr Mwananshiku knocked at our door and said, "The schools are opening in two weeks' time. I have managed to get you a bursary. Begin preparing for going back."

Though I thanked him, deep down in my heart I had doubts, thinking 'How can this man, a mere neighbour, be concerned with my problem? There must be a catch.' Later I learnt that the bursary was from the United National Independence Party, UNIP.

"Mulamu", I called, addressing my brother-in-law, "Mr Mwananshiku came to say he has succeeded with the bursary, but do you think he is just pulling my leg? If it is true, then what could be the reason behind all this concern and kindness?" I was suspicious.

"Yes, it is true he got you the bursary," Ephraim replied, "and his point is you are an intelligent girl who is always the top of the class, as we all in this neighbourhood know. You need help and support especially as you are not interested in the proposed marriage. I assure you there is nothing sinister behind all this.".

My own core-family having deserted me, why would I expect kindness from a total stranger? UNIP realised that talented young people needed to obtain qualifications that Zambia could draw on when Independence came; I was fortunate to have been singled out. My spirits were raised at the thought of returning to school, and the thought that it was just a matter of one year until I could enrol to become a Registered Nurse. I have never felt so grateful. My brother-in-law was a kind hearted person who quietly supported me and did everything he possibly could within his means to make the return to school a reality.

In primary school my dream had long been to go to Chipembi Secondary School. I was inspired by Chipembi girls such as Catherine Chileshe, Charity Kapotwe and Kekelwa Nyaywa, our headmaster's daughter in the neighbourhood. During school holidays I would catch glimpses of them, looking composed and confident as they walked, and chatted and I wanted to be like them. Chipembi Girls' Secondary School, run by Methodist missionaries, was the number one school for girls in the whole country in those days and many of its alumni went on to be prominent women.

When I was in my final year before entering secondary school, Mr Job Mutakwa, our Standard Six teacher was concerned about me and felt the need to pump some sense into me, because I was very naughty and playful. He called me to his office, and said, "You are a very intelligent girl but you are too playful and not serious with your studies. The coming final examinations are tough. Tell me, if you fail what are you going to do? Get married? I know you are top of the class but that is no guarantee when it comes to the coming examinations. You need to prepare adequately."

I took heed of his words. The examinations came and I passed, as they say with flying colours, and qualified for Chipembi. You can imagine how disappointed I was when I thought that I would have to give up my hard-earned place after just one year.

Chipembi, the school of my dreams

It was indeed an enormous pride to belong to this great missionary school. All the teachers came from Britain and for most of us it was our first encounter with white teachers. We had to adjust in many ways, especially when it came to the proper application of the Queen's language. Despite our consciousness that we were at an elite institution, we were not particularly well behaved! Like schoolgirls everywhere, we were inevitably curious about our teachers' love-lives, spying on the poor women when they had male visitors and happened to be on night duty. I remember when Eve, Violet, I and another girl whose name I can't remember, full of mischief, got out of the dormitory and followed a couple for a closer view. It was a narrow miss – the teacher and her partner must have heard our whispers or the rustling of the dry grass because at one point they stopped walking as though to listen. We lay low for a while then began to crawl on our bellies back to House 9, our dormitory. When the four of us held a post-mortem of the previous night's escapade we regretted our actions, not because it was reprehensible, but because it was sheer madness. Had we been found out it would have led to instant dismissal!

Standards were high at the school, and not just in class. We were expected to be responsible for our own cooking, and

I'll never forget the humiliation of revealing that, although I was nearly sixteen at the time, I hadn't the faintest idea how to cook nshima (so perhaps my mother wasn't always a slave driver?).

One thing about most of us who went to Chipembi in the late 1940s to 1960s is that we are very passionate about our former school and about each other. Most of us have done very well for the country and for ourselves. As a way of thanking our school ChiGAA (Chipembi Girls Alumni Association) continues to be very active, with an amazing membership of varying age. We love singing and still have beautiful voices. We still refer to ourselves as 'Chipembi Girls'. Even when we meet at various events, and some are using walking sticks or really struggling to walk we still refer to ourselves as 'Girls' in a loving way. Occasionally we sing at functions and events such as burials of our departed Chipembi friends. As a matter of fact each and every one of us is a torchbearer of progress individually.

In 1960, after two academic years, when I was waiting for my final exam results I received a visitor, someone I had never seen before. He introduced himself as Mr Nkonde. I later learnt that Mr Brahim Nkonde was one of the UNIP founding members. He said, "I am reliably informed that you intend to go for Nursing, and we wondered if you would be interested to take a course that is on offer in Germany."

"Germany! White people's land? No, no that is too far away, I would rather go to Mpilo Hospital in Bulawayo," I answered, shaking my head.

He explained that his daughter, Pelluny, had left two weeks previously for the same place, and he asked if I knew her. Yes, I knew her from Chipembi and decided that if Pelluny was there I would go too. I made this huge decision on impulse and without asking permission from anyone in my family. It was an opportunity not to be missed. Mr Nkonde told me I'd need to apply for a passport, then travel to Dar-es-Salaam by road and then fly to Berlin in Germany. He told me not to discuss this with anybody I did not trust, because the Government (still at this time British) must not know about my travel.

At this time there was a second 'scramble for Africa' between the global powers. Recognising that the British Empire was collapsing, America and the Soviet Union were keen to consolidate their influence and Britain was also thinking ahead to post-independence. There were more students going to Russia, East Germany, Yugoslavia, Bulgaria and Poland than those going to Britain, because British scholarships were very few; they did not wish us genuine development in Africa as these other countries did. This policy went right down to providing higher education to promising young African students; it was an unsung aspect of the 'cold war.'

My sister, her husband and I sat down to brainstorm and analyse the possibilities and constraints. Lack of resources topped the list. I needed a passport and that alone was thirty British shillings and transport to Dar-es-Salaam was two British pounds. All this was way beyond our means. Although secrecy was the order, it was felt that consultation of certain trusted individuals in the family was at this stage imperative. My brother-in-law had a cousin called Ida Mumbi, who was quite smart and enterprising, and it was agreed that she be approached about ways I might raise the necessary funds.

Because I sometimes made my own clothes, Ida offered to speak to her supervisor at Desco Clothing Factory to see whether I might be hired by them as a machinist. I'd never used a foot operated machine, but it was a valuable learning curve and I certainly needed the money to train as a nurse and to escape any more of my mother's marriage plans. Mother was kept in secret about Germany – she would have had a fit if she had known! It turned out to be a Godsent job, though in my first month I had to undo many garments I'd sewn, often barely achieving my daily target and then only with Ida's help.

17

It was not until I'd raised enough money to pay for my passport that a formal application was made. Mr Chalabesa at UNIP Secretariat advised me that 'Personal Secretary to Kenneth Kaunda the President of the Party UNIP' be used as my reason for travel and crossing into Tanganyika (as Tanzania was then called) would not raise any suspicion. My very first passport was, as a consequence a British one, citizen of the Protectorate of Northern Rhodesia and I even used it to get back home two years after Independence in 1966. If it were today, we would probably have concluded it was *kikikikiki* (corruption) to use Party connections in this way! By 1960, in contrast to the federal government's stance, British administrators were beginning to recognise UNIP for what it was, the banning order of 1959 had been lifted, leaders had been released from detention and independence was a realisable goal. The timing was just right for me.

Under the guidance, loving care and supervision of Ida, I worked at Desco Clothing from September to mid-December 1960, by which time I had enough money for the trip to Dar, but I still needed a suitcase, warm clothes, new shoes and pocket money before undertaking the trip to Germany. My brother, Lebby, could have been the right person to assist in purchasing those items as he had the financial capacity, but he was stingy, with an attitude. He also was not interested in my getting educated, and thus was not made privy to the pending trip – I didn't trust him after the marriage proposal incident, and I'd once had a very disheartening experience with him concerning money he'd promised for school fees. (Later, when I was successful his story changed). Once again I had to be inventive – I had an old tin trunk I'd used at Chipembi, so I approached a cousin who had a suitcase and he graciously and lovingly made a swop. For warm clothes my sister gave me a beautiful pleated, olive green skirt and a cream turtleneck pullover that complemented my navy blue Chipembi blazer. My brother-in-law bought me a pair of black shoes to complete my list of requirements. I found no words appropriate enough to thank my sister and her husband, and I shall continue to thank and pray for them for the rest of my life. Without them I would not be the person I am today. My gratitude to them is immense.

My dream comes true

The month for my trip was set for December 1960, at the peak of the rainy season. From Lusaka the bus took three-and-a-half days to reach Dar-es-Salaam because the gravel roads were so slippery. There were times when the driver would stop and request us passengers to disembark, especially on uphill stretches such as the Danger Hills of Mpika. I still clearly remember the scary conversation that took place amongst the passengers about the many human lives that the marauding lions of Danger Hills had taken. One man fantasized that right now a hungry, vicious old lion was lurking in the bush, wondering who to pounce on. Believing his story, I moved to the middle of the group where I felt shielded by bigger and taller passengers!

The first stop on Tanzanian [then still Tanganyika] soil was at Mbeya, where I was received by Mr Masaiti, the UNIP Representative. He booked me into a guesthouse close to their residence and later invited me for dinner at their home. In the guesthouse was another guest, a trade unionist on his way home from Europe who knocked at my door then barged into my room without waiting for my response. He introduced himself as someone from Northern Rhodesia who went to Europe for studies. I did not like the look of him and he was blind in one eye. He sat on the bed and invited me to sit next to him, which I declined; he stood up, grabbed me and a struggle ensued. My non-submissive character had to come out very strongly – with all the energy I could marshal, I kneed the man in the groin! Howling, he let go of me. I ran into the corridor, terrified and shaking like a

19

leaf, but when the manager, a man of Asian origin, saw me he was angry with me, not my assailant, shouting, "These are single rooms. You are not allowed to have visitors of the opposite sex."

He was accusing *me* of immoral behaviour. I was learning fast what it was to be a young woman alone in the world and I barricaded myself in my room for the rest of the night.

The second leg of the journey started the next day. I took a window seat which enabled me to watch the beautiful savannah scenery throughout the journey and I had a good view of the wildlife – impala, duiker and zebra. At Dar bus stop there was a pleasant surprise for me, I was thrilled to see that Abel Mkandawire, who used to be my partner during ballroom dancing lessons at Munali Secondary School, had come to welcome me in a foreign country. At that time Tanganyika was well on the road to full independence, which it would achieve as Tanzania, after incorporating Zanzibar, in 1964. The country already had majority rule and as such it welcomed freedom fighters and students from not only Northern Rhodesia but also Southern Rhodesia (Zimbabwe) and Nyasaland (Malawi) as well as South Africa. Munali was Chipembi's 'brother' school and provided many of the leaders in all fields after independence. The bus stop was a hustle and bustle of activity, thronged with more people and more merchandise than I had ever seen before in one place.

"How did you know I was coming?" I asked Abel.

"Actually I was not aware until this morning when Mr Kapasa Makasa, the UNIP Representative, called all of us guys and asked if any of us knew a girl called Selina from Lusaka. I could not think of any other Selina but you, so welcome to Dar es Salaam!"

Abel handed me over to Mr Kapasa Makasa who greeted me with the traditional warmth of an uncle. I now felt safe again after the difficult journey. He told me he would ask the Germans to confirm my flight and that there was another girl, Anna Mukuka Mbulo, who had just arrived from Kasama and would be travelling with me. Meanwhile, he had requested Ntombi, a lady from Southern Rhodesia, to accommodate both of us and asked me to check with him each morning.

Anna and I shared a room at Ntombi's for two weeks as we waited for our travelling formalities to be finalised. The first morning I went to present myself to Mr Makasa per his instructions, and he gave me a fatherly warning, "I will be very brief," he said. "I want to make it clear to you that you are here for a purpose, you are in transit to school, not for anything else. You are a very charming and attractive girl, but be very careful. Have you noticed how all those young men are clamouring for you? Each of them is wanting to make an impression on you, but if you give in you are doomed, finished. You get pregnant and you'll have to return to Lusaka, but the boy will have nothing to lose and he goes ahead with his education. I hope I have made myself clear."

Huuu! That was a mouthful of a lecture! Mr Makasa repeated the same fatherly advice daily for the two weeks that I stayed in Dar! I didn't really resent it, he made me feel loved, protected, and made me want to achieve my intended goal at all costs.

PART TWO

From Dar-es-Salaam to Berlin

On 31st December 1960, we boarded a Scandinavian Airlines System (SAS) plane. What an adventure – for the first time in my life I was up in the sky and I was going to Europe! Oh what a sensational feeling. It was an evening flight and as soon as we settled down dinner was served; but the flight was very bumpy, there was that feeling of having my insides pulled down and eating was just impossible. My travelling companion, Anna, became seriously airsick.

At 6.00 am on 1st of January 1961, the plane touched down at Berlin's Brandenburg Airport. The ground was all white. Neither of us had seen anything like it before and wondered what it was. When the doors opened icy cold air pushed in. Other passengers were warmly dressed in expensive coats of fur, leather or wool, but the two of us shivered in our thin clothing. I was a bit more warmly dressed than Anna, because I had a turtleneck and a blazer on, but she just had a short-sleeved cotton dress. Someone came to meet us, on board, and gave us each an oversized coat to hang over our shoulders. Everything was made so easy for us and after clearance we were taken to a hotel near the airport.

We couldn't believe the luxury we were led to – a double room with two single beds. On each was an envelope addressed to Anna and Selina, containing a welcome letter that included our programme for the following days. This being the festive season, the room was bright and colourful with decorations on a miniature Christmas tree. We were mesmerized by the beauty of the room. On one small table was a large bowl of assorted fruits: red and green apples, also red and green grapes, mandarins, bananas, oranges and a pineapple in the middle. There were beautiful pictures on the pastel wall paper. Waah! It was as though I was watching a movie! I'd never seen anything like it in Northern Rhodesia. There was even a glistening chandelier! The hotel room was warm and cosy with a beautiful view to the main street. Cars passed and a tramcar that we both referred to as a small train, because we had never seen one before. The hotel staff were very curious and they came in groups; one would touch my hair, another Anna's hair saying, 'Es ist weich, wie wolle', meaning it is soft like wool. For most of them this was probably their first encounter with a real African.

The welcome letter stated that we were expected to travel to our school on the 5th January as it was opening on the 7th. On the 4th an interpreter came to pick us up to go on a shopping spree for winter wear. Neither of us had ever seen such an exquisite and massive shopping complex; it had everything, but being of a small stature I found nothing to fit me in the ladies' section so I was referred to the children's department, where I found even nicer (and cheaper) garments. Anna and I walked out of the shop with our hands full of packages.

How different everything was from home.

"Hey look, Anna, the white men are working!" I exclaimed excitedly in my native language, pointing at four men dressed in blue overalls drilling in the road. It was inconceivable in Northern Rhodesia to see a white man doing manual work; there it was always the black man at work with a white man supervising, mostly with his hands in his pockets.

Back at the hotel there was excitement in the room as we tried on our new wardrobe. For the first time in both our lives we wore slacks. We were going to reinvent ourselves in this exciting new country.

The Quedlinburg School of Nursing

On 5th January 1961, a car came to take us on the four hour journey to Quedlinburg School of Nursing where Anna and I were pleasantly surprised to meet many other African students from Tanzania, Southern Rhodesia, Nigeria, Cameroon, Guinea, Mali and Senegal, also people from Cuba. All of us spoke different languages, English, French, Spanish or Portuguese, but as German would now be our medium of communication we all had to learn it for one year before starting the nursing course itself. There was a mixture of men and women; there were teenagers, like Anna and me, and mature people with families back home. German wasn't all we had to learn, many things were done differently from back at home and we had to adapt to a completely different way of life, and arriving in the depths of a European winter certainly brought its own problems.

Anna and I continued to share a room in the student hostel. One February morning I woke up at six to see that snow covered three quarters of my window, trees were all covered and the streets deserted. Anna and I concluded that as there was nobody to be seen on the street, there'd be no school. We snuggled back into our beds, but two hours later our teacher decided to check on the girls from Northern Rhodesia.

"Oh!" we said, "We woke up early alright, but when we saw so much snow and the streets deserted, we thought there would be no classes." Wrong again!

"Snow or no snow, work continues," she said. "I commute from a town 45 km away, but I am here!" We learnt yet another lesson about the German way of doing things.

German Cuisine

Often things seemed very alien and the German diet was particularly strange to us. It centred on Irish potatoes, boiled, mashed or baked, accompanied by pork, chicken, beef or lamb cooked in different ways. The food usually looked good enough but what our eyes saw was different in the mouth. They decided to try to make the menu more palatable for us by adding rice and we welcomed the change, but the German chefs found preparing rice that would be appealing to the African students challenging – it was always soggy or sheer porridge.

We foreign students held a meeting to discuss our plight because we felt starved and our sponsors were paying for what we did not consume. We resolved to ask that we take charge of our meal allowances and be individually responsible for cooking our main meals according to a rota in a hostel kitchenette. The school administration's reaction was apprehensive about these suggestions, believing that too much time would be spent queuing in food shops and cooking, at the expense of study time. (Talking of queues, one had to queue for everything in East Germany at that time and most items were rationed, from toilet paper to food.) As time went on fewer and fewer foreign students ate in the dining hall, most of us bought one-plate cookers to use in our rooms. When the school administration discovered this, they were even more alarmed, fearing fire, so finally they turned a rest room into a beautiful kitchenette for us. Most Africans eat nshima but give it different names – sadza, pap, or gari, but maize meal was unavailable locally. One student had a visitor who had been in Germany for four years and introduced us to semolina as an alternative. We were all thrilled with this discovery that finally helped improve our diet.

Amongst all those nationalities at this school with their different cuisines, I liked the Nigerian style of cooking best. I befriended Salome, and tagged onto her for everything related to cooking. She taught me what ingredients to buy and back in the kitchen she would show me how to make different dishes. My favourite was stewed pig trotters.

Nursing Training

After one academic year learning German, we joined the first year group of German girls and boys for the nursing course proper. The first six months were spent on the theoretical syllabus and it was not easy taking notes as the lecturers spoke so fast. It meant leaving gaps for missing words and at times the sentence was not making sense. Back at the students' hostel one would ask friends and compare notes to make corrections, but as time went by our understanding of the language improved. We got used to the lecturers' fast talk and foreign students began performing very well, often better than many of the German students. I suspect this was not only because we had been hand-picked in our home countries, but also because we knew just how important our training was, not just for ourselves but also for our countries.

When the second part of training, namely 'practical', started there was excitement on the part of the students but more so for the patients for being cared for by African nurses. They were bubbling and full of questions such as:

"How did you come this far?"

"By airplane," we'd reply.

"It cannot be true. Africa has no planes or airports; all there is are thick forests and jungles so no plane can land," they would argue.

Another one would say:

"I want to see and touch the skin loin cloth you wore before they bought you our German clothes when you landed at Berlin airport."

"Tell me how does a family keep together up in the trees at night, especially babies, is there no danger of falling and sustaining injuries?"

Did they really believe that Africans lived up in trees like monkeys for lack of houses? Yes.

"Why are your palms lighter than other parts of the body, is it because of climbing trees?"

Any logical answer given was not good enough. We could not believe that Europeans could be so ignorant about Africa and her people in the 20th century! No pulling of leg - they were genuine. It was repeated by many even on the street. One would politely stop you just to touch you and ask such questions. I would say, "All this happened in winter, since the seas and oceans were frozen I simply used roller skating up to the beach."

"*Vunderbar*" they'd cheer.

On our course the practicals were getting more and more interesting. We foreign students had not yet mastered the psychology of the senior members of staff in the wards, but the German students were very good at that. When all was quiet, with neither routine nor emergency at hand, the foreign students would pull a chair and sit down, all of us did that, without exception, but the Germans would put up a show of 'acting busy' moving up and down the ward. The foreign students found this very strange and deceptive, but German students received very high marks in practical work for their fake busy-ness.

Back in class the foreign students were very serious and consistently had better grades than most German students in both nursing and medical theory. There was a German girl who sat on my right side and had a habit of copying from me; that got out of hand. The weekly test was every Friday and one time out of mischief I deliberately wrote trash, and exposed that to her. As usual she would copy anything without thinking it through. I later took a fresh piece of paper and wrote sense. At last the teacher saw who really was excelling.

Curiosity

In this small town of Quedlinburg, within a year it became common to see a coloured baby in a perambulator. Some of the German girls had gone crazy over the African men. One girl decided to open up and asked me, "Why is it that you African girls are not getting pregnant but we are?"

In my opinion the answer is simple. CURIOSITY!!

"Firstly," I said, "you want to experiment and find out whether truly a black man can sire, or see how does his male organ look. The English saying goes, 'curiosity killed the cat'. Secondly, we came to school and not to make babies." At the same time, most mature male African students had families back home but were promising marriage to these naïve, innocent girls who imagined a greater life out of the German Democratic Republic.

Sadly one girl after graduating excitedly migrated to Mali with her new husband, just to learn the hard way that she was the third wife, and they all had to live under one roof. The life she narrated was such a nightmare that she could not bear it. There was no running water, she had to draw water from the well, or from the river and being the youngest wife she was expected to do certain chores, serving the senior wives as well as the husband according to the culture. The husband was posted to a rural Health Centre and she did not even know how to get through to the German Embassy in Bamako, the capital city of Mali. She was cut off entirely, with no telephone. She swallowed her pride, wrote and asked for help from her parents who wrote to the Embassy which facilitated her return to Germany, a very bitter, but wiser, person.

Terrified and Smelled Death

One of my most memorable and scary encounters was when I went to the Baltic Sea for the 1962 summer holiday with a group of friends. There were five of us, three men from Mali and two women from Northern Rhodesia. The beaches were overcrowded but clean, with white sand for miles. One of the men from Mali asked whether I'd like to go out in a boat and when I asked whether they knew how to row he assured me that they did.

I asked Anna to join us. The two men rowed while we sat relaxing, admiring the sea-green colour of the water as we chatted in our mother language. The sea was unusually calm. The two men were talking in Bambara, their native language, but I could sense they were arguing, though I did not know over what. I thought to myself, "Katongo it is none of your business." Suddenly I noticed the danger marker on the water, a line to warn all those venturing beyond it that they are going there at their peril.

"Please let us go back, we have gone beyond the safe zone," I begged.

Our communication was in German because the two men came from a French-speaking country and spoke no English and we spoke no French either. It was as though my request fell on deaf ears. Then Kamisa, one of the rowers, dropped a bombshell saying, "My sister we are failing to turn the boat."

"What? You lied, when you said you knew how to row?"

I looked down into the depths of the sea, was terrified and smelled death. My stomach felt empty, as if I had not eaten for many days; the little swimming capability I had was not enough for situations like this. All I could think of were headlines in the daily German newspapers reading: *Four foreign students perish in the Baltic Sea during an adventure, two girls from Northern Rhodesia and two men from Mali!* What a way to end! I lamented.

I saw a small boat in the distance and I shouted for help. They came fast but that fast was not fast enough for me. Anna was so petrified she could not even utter a word. I told the guys in the rescuing boat that I would be the first to go on board. They got us safely back to the beach but I learnt a great lesson, not to be trusting or gamble with my life with people I do not know well.

I have always been a great lover of water, hence the attraction of a seaside resort for a holiday, while other fellow African students preferred to visit historical buildings such as castles, monuments, statues, or to stay at school and save themselves some money. Wherever we were, or whatever we were doing, as African students we attracted attention. I was at the beach attempting to swim, and three young boys aged between eight and ten were watching me struggle to float; they came closer and said *"Tante kuck mal,"* meaning 'Aunt, look!' One of them demonstrated how to use the arms and legs simultaneously and thereby float. They instantly became my swimming instructors; one of them took hold of my arms, another held my midriff and the third one my legs, without my realizing they let go and I continued swimming on my own, for quite a distance. I only realized I was on my own when they all clapped and shouted *"Vunderbar Tante"* meaning, 'Wonderful, Aunt!' That is how I learnt how to swim properly; my little German 'nephews' taught me how in the waters of the Baltic Sea.

Career Choice

During our schooldays we did not have informed career advice or mentors, therefore thinking of a career did not come easily for me. Initially I wanted to be a teacher so that I teach and beat the teachers' children! I was very naughty and did so many wrong things that a week did not pass without being given punishment of some sort, but as I grew older I realised how silly I was being and teaching as a career was shelved. The infatuation with the idea of becoming a nurse was now stronger, but when I look back either way my motives for becoming a nurse were equally flimsy – I liked the uniform and I liked the way the nurses walked, but I knew absolutely nothing about the nitty-gritty of the career. At that time girls' choices were limited, one became either a teacher, a nurse or a housewife.

During my training as a nurse I began having doubts as to whether I was carved out for nursing. The German authorities were very considerate over our training, they changed many things in the syllabus to include subjects that are usually only taught to doctors, knowing well that Africa lacked medical personnel and that nurses find themselves handling cases that in other countries are only performed by qualified doctors. The time came for our class to attend a laparotomy (opening up the abdomen). In theatre we all surrounded the operating table as observers; the surgeon took the scalpel and slit the skin, GUSH! Out oozed the blood. ZOOM, THUMP! I fainted. They took me out of theatre – that was the first and last time I entered an operating theatre during my nursing career.

The Marriage that Never Was

In 1963, whilst still in Germany, I married Fred Chella, a Zambian engineering student in Dresden. We had been dating for eighteen months. Fred loved his 'bottle', but during our dating period he would pretend to have stopped drinking. Because we lived in different towns, and I was very naïve, I believed him. The truth came out when I moved to Dresden to do my midwifery and discovered the real Fred. When advised to take less to the bottle he would brag, "The Chella family are known to be great beer drinkers. In fact, one of my uncles won a trophy for being the best beer drinker, therefore no one can convince me to stop."

As a child I could not stand the stench of beer, though I found myself in a very awkward situation where Mum was sending me to the tavern against my wishes to buy the opaque beer for her. The other thing I disliked at the tavern was when the drunken old men, and the younger ones too, would touch me with their scruffy hands, feeling my bum which I hated, as I felt abused and degraded. The smell of beer has always been and will always be offensive to me, be it opaque or lager. That was it, the marriage was over before it had really begun.

.

PART THREE

Back Home, Sweet Home (1966)

Now qualified nurses, we returned to Zambia. En route our first transit was Cairo in Egypt, but we missed our connecting flight to Zambia via Dar-es-Salaam so, to kill time, we decided to go sightseeing and also have a ride on a camel.

While we were in Egypt we decided to visit the pyramids. Pelluny's fiancé, Gef, attended a University in Cairo, and that meant we didn't need a guide or an interpreter. As we walked towards the pyramids an Egyptian man placed himself in front of us and kept looking behind over his shoulder for quite some distance. When we reached the foot of the pyramid, he turned round stretched his hand and said, "Pay me - I was your guide leading the way to the pyramids."

We could not believe such craftiness existed in this world, but he insisted that we pay for his services. Gef had to shut him up.

Home at Last

There is no place like home! In August 1966, we landed at Lusaka's old airport – I'd been away for five-and-a-half-years, during which both I, and my country, had changed a great deal. My brother-in-law and my sister were there to welcome me. While I was in Germany I had changed my name from Selina to Katongo. Being away from home had led to self-discovery and I was now questioning a lot of things, including why I should be answering to a white person's name when the whites rarely give their children our African names, no matter how long they live in Africa. I had to bribe my little nephews and nieces to call me Aunt Katongo, instead of Aunt Selina. (If they forgot and used the old name, they got no sweets!)

Starting Work

Within two weeks of arriving home we were sent to work at Kitwe Central Hospital. In those days there was plenty of employment for trained people. All Zambian nationals who were outside the country before Zambia became independent were expected to come back home and serve Mother Zambia. In most cases they were on scholarships initiated by the UNIP political party. The government had a long list of all students overseas and when they would graduate. We nurses reported to the Ministry of Health where we introduced ourselves to the personal secretary of Dr Nalumango, Permanent Secretary, Ministry of Health. She warmly greeted us but told us they had been expecting us the previous week and asked where we'd been – of course, the answer was Cairo! She gave us documents to fill in and sign, told us about our Kitwe posting and how to get our settling in allowance. She genuinely made us feel valuable to our Mother Zambia. It was a good feeling to know things had changed for the best; we'd left as Northern Rhodesians with Europeans as civil servants and now were back home as Zambians, finding fellow Zambians in charge.

The sunshine girls

At Kitwe Central Hospital I was assigned to the Non-Fee Paying Children's Ward and I enjoyed working with the toddlers and babies. There were three rotas to be accomplished in a month, morning, afternoon and night shifts. We were only six Zambian Registered nurses in the hostel, plus one married woman who lived outside the hospital grounds, making seven of us for the entire hospital.

The majority of nurses were whites, referred to as 'sunshine girls'. Why 'sunshine'? After independence in 1964 the Zambian government embarked on recruiting younger nurses, some fresh from UK colleges, for a two year contract. We called them 'sunshine girls' because all they did during their spare time was sunbathe, either by the swimming pool or on the balcony.

Shortly after independence there was still a lot of discrimination by the Whites and, on the other hand, most Zambians still considered themselves second class citizens, which is what the Whites had instilled into their minds over the years of colonialism. So to some extent they were scared of their white workmates, the concept of equality, human rights and freedom had not yet sunk in most of their heads. I can cite several examples.

The six of us State Registered nurses ate at the Sisters' mess where all the food was western. One day I made a suggestion to my colleagues that the Matron be approached and requested to allow the kitchen staff at the Sisters' mess to cook *nshima* for us; everyone agreed that it was a good idea. I had just joined this group so we asked Chibungo, who was much senior, to be the emissary, but she declined. I felt very strongly that something was just not right. How could we be eating western food in our own country, not by choice but by imposition, deprived of our traditional foods? I had just arrived from Germany craving delicacies such as *kalembula, kapenta,* dry roasted fish, *chibwabwa, kadingi.* The list of things I wanted to eat again was endless, so I made an appointment to see the Matron on behalf of the group. It went something like this:

ME: Matron, I have come on behalf of my colleagues. We request that *nshima* be cooked for the six of us.

MATRON: May I know the names of the interested sisters?

[I provided the names.]

MATRON: Sister Mulenga, I will get back to you after talking to the other sisters.

Two days later

MATRON: Sister Mulenga, please have a seat. I spoke to all those on the list that you gave me and they deny having had such discussion because they have no complaint about the food. In fact they love the food and are very happy.

Sister Mulenga, do I take it that you created this lie and then involved others?

I could not believe my ears. If I were a European my face would have turned crimson red.

ME: Matron, I do not know what to say, neither do I know what to think of the five. Miss Perry, let me ask you just one question. I am told you have been in Zambia long enough, five years or perhaps more, during this period have you even one single day eaten *nshima*?

Her face turned red and her blue piercing eyes narrowed.

MATRON: Sister Mulenga you are now being cheeky. How dare you ask me such a personal question?

ME: I just want to bring it to your attention that denying us *nshima* is neither fair nor right. The way you love your Irish potatoes is the way we love and enjoy our *nshima*.

MATRON: Sister Mulenga you can go.

ME: Matron thank you for your time.

I could not believe what my 'friends' had done to me. How could they betray me in such a manner, make her believe it was my machination and allow me to be ridiculed in such a way? I spoke to each one of them individually and expressed my disgust at their cowardice, betrayal and pretence. Deep down in their hearts they wanted *nshima* badly, but they were scared when confronted by the white boss. Their cowardice and inferiority complex was at centre stage.

The following week I went to town and bought myself a one-plate electric cooker, two small pots, a frying pan, cutting knife and some plates for use in my room, so that I could enjoy my *nshima* with whatever relish I fancied. One day I bought a kipper, after cooking *nshima* I took the kipper for grilling in the main kitchen grill, the tantalizing aroma of the smoked fish was all over. Two of my colleagues came to my room and one of them said: *"Awe apapenabonseepotuli"* (We are joining you).

It was my chance to remind them that it might have been months ago but I had not forgotten the ridicule I went through due to their cowardice, inconsistency and fear. "No way! What would the Matron think of you, if she found you eating stinking fish and *nshima* of all things?" I asked sarcastically. One of them was fast, washed her hands to start eating, pretending she did not take in my sarcasm. Since I was already full, I took the *nshima* and fish, stepped on the trash can peddle and threw them in. I guess they got the message loud and clear.

As I mentioned earlier, most 'sunshine girls' lacked experience, particularly knowledge of tropical diseases (or if it comes to that, nursing in general). During night shift the Matron would brief the white nurses that if they faced challenges they should contact Sister Mulenga for help. At the beginning I used to oblige and help with taking blood, putting up drips, nasal tubes and inserting catheters, etc. But soon I realized I was being used and taken for granted. As Zambians, we were paid less than the 'sunshine girls' who were on contract. Here I was, trained in Europe just like them, but because of being a Zambian my remuneration was far less. To make things worse those same girls despised and looked down upon us blacks, which to me was just not acceptable. The night shift was due again, the expatriate nurse, having had the usual directive from the Matron, 'Any problem, contact Sister Mulenga to assist,' was surprised when I simply told her I was not available.

"But those are instructions from Matron," she protested, believing it was her right.

"Oh yes, I understand and appreciate that, but please tell the Matron I said I am not available."

The next morning the Matron summoned me to her office and told me she had a report from Sister Y that I was not available to render assistance.

"Yes, Miss Perry, it is true and these are my reasons: I am not a teacher or tutor; Sister Y was trained in Europe and so was I; This is her first working place and this is also my first working place after training."

I put it to her that, in all fairness, it was not in order that I continue to do Sister Y's work, asking why she was hired if she had to depend on others to perform her duties? Matron once again turned red in the face and spluttered, "Sister Mulenga you are just impossible!"

Savings

One day four of us Zambian nurses were relaxing in Lizzie's room and I said to her, "I want you to show me your bank account balance, you have been working for a year so what are the savings like?"

After protesting that it was a private matter, she eventually complied when I said I wanted to use her as a guideline to what I could set aside. When she showed me her savings book I was shocked. There was just £75 sterling. What on earth did she do with her money when accommodation and food were free?

My first salary was £50 sterling per month, after deductions. My long standing goal and dream was to dress up Daddy, as well as Mum, from head to toe. During some nights off my boyfriend, Abe Maine drove me to Lusaka. On opening the suitcase I had brought her, Mum was ecstatic; she could not believe what she saw – every piece of clothing she once would have wished for was there. You could feel the excitement; she was like a child and could not hide her feelings and I could not resist saying, "Hey Mum! I am happy that you like my choice, but can you imagine if you had succeeded in marrying me off all those years ago to that good for nothing pauper? All this would not have been there. I would have been just as poor as him - if not poorer."

Taking the Risk

From childhood, I have always had this thought at the back of my mind that I deserved the best, something special in my life, be it working conditions, salary, relationships and in general living. My close friend was Pelluny Nkonde and, both of us having been trained in Germany, we felt £50 sterling per month was not sufficient for us. We were still searching for better opportunities and concluded that the only way was to resign from government and join 'the Mines'. The government was already putting restrictions on such movements of professionals, but we decided to risk it. The question was how both of us could resign at the same time without raising eyebrows?

We applied to the Mines and employment was offered, but we could not start immediately as we were required to give three months' notice to the Civil Service Commission. We told our new employers that we had just arrived from Germany and that we could only start work after three months.

I approached Matron and asked for a transfer to Kabwe General Hospital, as our strategy was to give the impression that the two resignations were not linked. I applied a lot of pressure on Matron knowing well that, since I was not in her good books anyway, she would heave a sigh of relief to see me go. I submitted my letter of resignation immediately. I started work in Kabwe and from there I moved to the Ronald Ross Hospital in Mufulira.

Ronald Ross Hospital

Starting work at Ronald Ross Hospital in Mufulira unfolded its own challenge as we anticipated that our cover up would, some day, be exposed by an old schoolmate who was the only Zambian Registered Nurse at the hospital. Sure enough this happened, though she didn't realise what she was letting us in for when she responded honestly to Matron's direct questioning.

Matron confronted us asking why we had lied about our government contracts in our applications. We apologised but explained in full and asked to be forgiven – we were referred to the personnel officer to explain ourselves. After a bit of obligatory bluster, Mrs McPherson, the manager told us, "You have been forgiven, and what has truly saved you is the fact that you are both darn good at your work. The doctors and those in charge of you are very happy with your performance. By the way, is there anything else you told us which was not true?"

"No Madam, the rest is the truth and we thank you very much for giving us a second chance," I replied meekly.

I remember one familiarization tour we had of the underground mine. I was the only Zambian. This was shortly after the Unilateral Declaration of Independence of Southern Rhodesia, led by Ian Smith, and all the shift bosses were white, from Southern Rhodesia. When tea was offered the question was: "How do you want it - 'Rhodesian' or 'Zambian'?"

Proud of being a free Zambian; I said "I will have Zambian!"

Of course, the others said "Rhodesian".

When the tea was served, mine was the only black tea. Defiantly I drank it anyway. The discrimination was there but in a more subtle way, unlike at the government hospital where all was obvious and the blacks still had to dance to the tune. This, I did not accept.

When I left Kitwe Central Hospital I promised myself my own car, and told my workmates to expect I'd have it within six months. The work was good and so was the money. Working for the Mines was enjoyable, even the 'sunshine girls' there displayed respect, and a good comradely attitude. I opted to work the afternoon and night shifts, where the remuneration was pegged higher.

My First Brand New Car

True to my word, come six months I went to an Ndola car dealer and put down a deposit towards the hire purchase of a Datsun 1000. When my nights off were due, I drove to Kitwe to show off my new car to my former workmates. Lizzie thought it must be my boyfriend's, then couldn't believe it was mine, wondering how I'd afforded it when I started work after them. What she did not realize was that we were no longer on the same salary scale.

Yes, of course I knew they would say it was Abe's, so I pulled out the ownership 'blue' book and asked, "Does this read Katongo Mulenga or not?"

I got my first driver's licence in Germany, in 1965, before even graduating as a midwife. I used to visualize driving a car, not necessarily a specific car, just any car. My first goal had been achieved. I was on course and patted myself on the shoulder, "KATONGO - well done girl and congratulations!!"

How does it Feel to be Drunk?

My stay at Ronald Ross Hospital in Mufulira was short, but memorable, with many treasured experiences. The New Year's Eve of January, 1968, Pelluny and I were bored. My boyfriend had travelled to South Africa to be with his family for Christmas. We were the only two Zambian Nursing Sisters in the Mess and in a spirit of rebellion I announced, "Hey Pelluny, don't you think we are now old enough to experiment and find out how it feels to be drunk?"

She agreed it would be an interesting experience, so we asked our friend, Gef to tell us what drinks women take which do not stink or taste bitter. He advised sherry or Cinzano, neat. I argued I'd buy Fanta and coca cola, to make it sweet, because I do not like bitter things.

"How do you know it is bitter before you even taste it? That is why you Africans end up too drunk because of wrong mixtures," he commented sarcastically with a Mr-Know-it-all attitude.

We bought what we were advised to buy (Fanta and Coca Cola included) and Gef bought himself a bottle of Johnny Walker whisky. Gef and I were drinking and playing cards and Pelluny was just guzzling down the stuff. Within a very short time she became drunk and quarrelsome, but the drink only got hold of me close to midnight. I felt I needed some fresh air because my head had begun to spin. I went out and sat on the veranda, all by myself and began to laugh continuously for quite some time.

My neighbour, a 'sunshine girl' came to find out what the matter was and I looked at her and continued to giggle. She lifted me up, and led me to my room, put me on my bed and I continued to giggle myself to sleep. When I woke up the next morning I had a splitting headache, foul mouth and felt fatigued. All I could remember was the giggling. I wondered where the joy of getting drunk was, if this is all it is, it is not for me ever again!

At Ronald Ross Hospital I worked in the Out Patient Department and Male Medical Ward, then the Children's Ward. One incident left an indelible mark on my mind. In the Male Medical Ward we admitted a patient in great pain and with difficulty in swallowing solids. The condition got worse, but the doctor-in-charge kept prescribing analgesics. Once every month there came a visiting surgeon as consultant from Salisbury (Harare) Southern Rhodesia and I expected that particular patient to be on his list. The following visit the patient still did not qualify for the Specialist List. Since I was assigned to work with the visiting consultant I used that opportunity to request him to examine the patient, despite his not being on the list. He asked why I felt so strongly about this man and I explained that he was getting worse and his symptoms were those of cancer of the oesophagus.

The consultant confirmed my diagnosis, asked how long I'd been nursing and where I'd been trained, complimenting me on my very thorough East German training. The patient's treatment was changed to morphine injection but it was too late for surgery. Shortly after that I was transferred to the Children's Ward, but the patient would only accept to be given injection by Sister Mulenga because he claimed her injections were not painful. This kind of behaviour is typical of many terminally ill patients. Every injection time the staff had to call me and would make fun of it and say, "Your patient is ready for injection." He had become my patient, not our patient collectively!

Married Life

Fred had made me very wary about marriage. He had an affair with a German girl – it was not a matter of hearsay, I found him with her myself, so asked for a divorce. Although I had given up on Fred long before I knew of the affair, finding out the truth was painful and I was indeed heartbroken. Fred used to drink like ten devils, and this upset me a lot. When he became too much of a nuisance, I told him it was over. When he heard this he attempted suicide - twice. One time he jumped out of a fast moving tram-car and on the other occasion he set fire to himself. Both times the German police had to interrogate me, although we lived separately in Students Hostels according to our faculties. I was scared stiff and disoriented and forgave him both times, but he never changed, so finding him with the girl was a great blessing in disguise for me.

With Abe it was a different story, I loved him with a burning love and I believed he loved me equally; we were both mature and to crown it all he did not indulge in alcohol and for this I loved him even more. Abe came from South Africa to escape the *apartheid* regime and we met at Kitwe Central Hospital through a friend of his, Neb Jere. Abe was a very nice, quiet and pleasant person whom I liked immediately, but I did not take him seriously, meaning I did not want to get involved in another love affair, having not very long ago been disappointed with my short-lived marriage in Germany. The most important thing that impressed me was his kindness, sincerity and respect for women. It is hard to find such in the relationships of today's younger generation.

In 1968 I conceived, but for me marriage was out of the question as I did not want to be heartbroken once more. I loved Abe dearly, but was confused and didn't really know what I wanted, but one thing I was sure about was that I wanted the baby and would call him Ralesite Junior. Abe insisted that we marry, but I was still so shaken and spiritually hurt that my thinking was all negative and somehow warped. One day he said, "Well, you are wrong when you say all men are bad. Give me a chance to show you that I am different."

I gave him the chance and for sure I enjoyed, appreciated, cherished and loved his company for many years to come, till death did us part. May his Soul rest in eternal peace.

Somehow, I had never liked the idea of being pregnant in a nurse's uniform, so I resigned from Ronald Ross Hospital, and started playing the role of housewife and enjoyed pampering my husband. In December, 1968 we married and I moved back to Kitwe where Abe worked at Zambia National Broadcasting Corporation Kitwe Studios, in the newsroom. We were very happy together, still madly in love with each other. Ralesite, our first son, was born the year that followed. We were very grateful to each other for being able to bring such a lovely little creature into the world, and Abe was most proud.

I Loved Seeing Myself in Beautiful Clothes

In 1969, Abe left for Columbia University in New York, meaning that we had to vacate our government house, situated on Independence Avenue in Kitwe. Musonda my four-year-old niece, my fourteen-year-old sister Beatrice and I moved into a very big mine house, in Nkana West with baby Ralasite. It was sparsely furnished with only basic necessities. I had returned to work at Wusakile Hospital and was supporting the family. In our Zambian family set up it was the normal thing to take care of your younger siblings, nephews or nieces and I believe it still is once you have your own home; you help to educate them, hence my younger sister and my niece came under my care. Our son was growing very fast and was strikingly handsome and clever for his age; he made me a proud mother when people passed comments on what a good-looking boy he was.

I was not sure the Americans would allow me to join my husband, so it was a worrying time. Abe had a very small scholarship that covered only his tuition. He approached the Dean of Students and explained that his wife was a professional, and if permitted to work then that problem would be overcome. The Dean said he would help with the relevant documents that were needed for my work permit, but Columbia University itself had no job to give me.

Everything was so uncertain, but after five months (which to me seemed like five years) I resigned from Wusakile Hospital and followed Abe. Before the departure to New York I received a parcel from him that contained a thick jersey, a hat and gloves all in preparation for the forthcoming winter trip; it made me realise that we really were going to live in the United States.

One evening in the mine house I was bathing Rali, while Bee and Musonda watched TV. I heard an alarming scream from the sitting room, hurriedly wrapped the baby in the towel laid him on the bed and ran out to see what the problem was. I found Musonda still screaming at the top of her voice and assumed that Bee had hit her. It turned out that she'd seen an old, wrinkled woman on TV and was horrified that she might one day look like that. I told her that someday we'll all be old, whether we like it or not and she started to cry. At that time you didn't see many old women in the towns of Zambia.

Later I asked Musonda why she did not want to be old like that old woman.

"I do not want to be old because if I do, you will not make me nice dresses," she explained with that child's innocence.

I liked making my own outfits and each time I made some garment I also made something fancy for Musonda out of the same material. I enjoyed trying new exciting creations, and in general I love seeing myself in beautiful clothes and it seemed she had taken after me. Little were either of us to realise how important dressmaking would be to our family one day.

The preparations for the trip to the USA were so involved that many journeys had to be made between Kitwe and Lusaka before the American Embassy could issue us a visa. I would start off from Kitwe as early as 5.30 a.m., drop our son at Mindolo Ecumenical Centre with a friend, Edith Grenville Grey. By 9.00 a.m. I would be in Lusaka. Each time I telephoned to check on the baby, Edith's comment would be, "Ha! Already in Lusaka! That is too fast, please drive and not fly."

46

In those old days the government had certain conditions for citizens leaving the country who were self-sponsored; importantly, one had to deposit enough money in the bank for the return air ticket in case things did not go well abroad and the Zambian Government had to repatriate. In real terms, air fares were much more expensive in those days than they are now and the fares to New York were already astronomical without having to match them with the required indemnity. At this stage my resources were much depleted, as the tickets had been purchased and visas paid for.

Mr and Mrs. Gaobepe who were Abe's adopted parents came all the way from Kasama where they taught at Kasama Teachers College to see me and our son off to America. These were kind, loving, considerate and generous people who originated from South Africa as Abe did. In 1964 when he'd arrived in Zambia for a journalism course at Mindolo they were the first South Africans he met in Kitwe, and they warmly welcomed him. When they asked how my plans for the trip were going, I told them that everything was in place except the cash guarantee to the government for me and Rali.

I left the sitting room to make some tea and when I came back with the tray Mee Gaobepe told me that they had decided then and there to provide the required money so that their son Abe could have his family with him. What a loving gesture! I was humbled and very grateful that the biggest hurdle had been overcome just when I was beginning to despair, because I truly did not know who, or where to turn to. I promised to pay them back from my first paycheck.

Our flight was via London, and at Lusaka Airport I noticed something very interesting, a white lady, carrying her baby on her back the Zambian way. She looked comfortable and in control of the situation – I admired her style. There I was with my heavy baby in a carrycot in the western way, overwhelmed and struggling to manage various bits of hand luggage.

"Why on earth did I not have my baby on my back like her?" I mourned to myself.

On arrival at J F Kennedy Airport a porter assisted me with my baggage and I thanked him for being a gentleman. I stood there next to my son's baby cot and suitcases waiting for my husband's arrival and the guy also stood there staring at me to the point where I felt uncomfortable. After a while he came closer, and in a husky voice said, "Next time you must remember that this is how I earn my living."

Coming from Zambia at the height of Humanism, I was at a loss because the guy seemed to be asking for a bribe (in Zambia at the time tipping was illegal) but here in a capitalist society it was a legitimate source of income which I was not aware of. Under Humanism you were employed to do a job and expect no further reward.

The New York Job

Here I was, a complete stranger in New York, needing to earn enough money to support our little family, but it has never been in my nature to be overwhelmed by circumstances. I made an application to Mount Sinai Hospital in Manhattan, which was within walking distance from where we lived. After interviews they told me they first wanted to hear from my school in Germany. Two weeks later they called me and offered me a job. The lady said, "You seem to have been a darn good student. The report is excellent, we are happy to have you."

However, in the end I did not take up the offer because I was meant to do all three shifts, morning, afternoon and night and that would not give me the chance for attending school - I wanted to take advantage of my time in New York to train as a fashion designer. Although our financial situation had reached an alarming point of desperation, it was in my interest that I hang on for a better option. I said to myself, 'Katongo, if you accept this job offer out of fear of destitution that will be the end of the dream to change your career from nursing'.

Meanwhile I applied to two more hospitals and sent word round to our American friends that if they heard of any job opportunity they should let us know. One day one of them, Polly Woodard, gave me a contact number that resulted in a nursing position at the Sheridan House Drug Rehabilitation Center; that was ideal in that it required only evening shifts, allowing me to go to school during the day.

I was glad to be working again, not just for the money but also because I was able to train as a fashion designer. The flat we occupied was very small, just a sitting room/ kitchen, small bedroom, shower and toilet. When it was house-cleaning time it took me less than 20 minutes to complete everything. The rest of the day I was just watching television.

After the interview at the centre I was asked when I wanted to start work.

"Tomorrow!" was my prompt answer, "But I have a request to make. Is it possible that I work only afternoon shift to enable me go to school in the morning?"

"Oh yes; this slot is meant for afternoon only," the lady said.

Was I happy! And what a relief! I was joyous and grateful to God that at long last I had got what I needed and wanted and thank God that I had good qualifications that were recognized anywhere in the world. I had found a good child-minder and was delighted to start work. When I received my first cheque I went to enrol at Traphagen School of Fashion. From my first cheque I also paid back the Gaobepes the guarantee money they had lent me.

The 4% Sales Tax

The new income was a great blessing, it saved me from an embarrassing situation that had begun to haunt me each time I went to buy our weekly groceries. Abe would give me a certain amount meant for the purchases. I would list down each item and sum up the total, but at the till I would have to take out some items because it was always more than I had calculated, at times I was taking out that which was most needed in panic. I began dreading my grocery day, since I frequented the same supermarket. Abe asked me if I was taking into account the 4% sales tax? That said it all!

Due to our tight budget I used to buy only chicken necks and backs, we considered wings a great treat. Student life can be hard!

When I received my pay, we both thought I'd been overpaid and I was afraid that if there'd been an error I might fail to be able to reimburse it. I took the cheque back for clarification and it turned out that as a foreigner on temporary basis I was exempt from most deductions. What a relief that was. The money I earned took care of all our needs – rent, my school fees, groceries, the child minder, our clothing and our few trips out of town.

We once were visited by an old acquaintance from home in Kitwe who said he could not even temporarily permit the situation that prevailed in our home, where the wife was the breadwinner, while the husband went to school. I simply thought he was a male chauvinist pig! In our marriage we were a true partnership and I was proud to be able to help my husband achieve his goals.

My daily routine ran like clockwork: I used to take our son to the child minder's home before I went to Traphagen School of Fashion from 9.00 a.m. to 3pm, then from 4pm to midnight I worked at the Narcotic Control Centre. I found designing very interesting, and because I loved what I was doing it was all smooth sailing. Abe picked up our son after his classes.

After work I used to be scared stiff walking so late at night to and from the bus stop; at that time New York City had just too much crime. Abe once suggested he meet me at the bus stop but that would mean leaving our son on his own in the flat. If anything happened to both of us while out there then Rali would be alone in this harsh and cruel world. We both dearly loved our son, so we opted for me to continue to find my way home alone. Somehow, God sent a proxy companion, who came on the bus one stop after me; this man and I dropped off at the same place as he lived in the block across the road. America being such an unfriendly country neither of us ever uttered a word to the other, but strangely I felt very safe and protected in his company despite his white cane. He was blind. I would at times be in deep thought wondering why the blind people back home don't hold regular jobs like this man; instead they opt to perpetually remain street beggars.

I very much appreciated the American community's respect for uniformed personnel, in particular nurses. Each time I jumped on the bus or underground train someone would offer their seat and say, "Give the seat to the nurse. She has been on her feet the whole day."

Due to our tight programmes Abe and I rarely had time to socialize with our fellow Zambians, but one of the diplomats at the New York Zambian Mission once invited us to his home and we met many Zambians, the ladies confronting me with a barrage of criticism of my lifestyle.

Why do you go to school

"Why do you go to school and go to work full-time as well, how is it possible?"

"When do you sleep?"

"What is the matter with you? Why have you turned yourself into a slave in a foreign country?"

"Hey relax! This is New York, enjoy yourself."

Before I could answer another one would say, "I am told you work from Monday to Sunday, ha! Even if it is for the love of money I can't subject myself to that, no way."

Then it was another and another comment. I got the impression that this was not the first time I was being discussed and was irritated and said, "Ladies, I want you to appreciate that all of you here came on a Government of

Republic of Zambia ticket, but I had to buy the two tickets for me and for our son. Obviously from the outset you can tell that my mission and goals are different from yours. For me, going to school is a matter of life and death. At the same time, if I do not work I cannot go to school. As for turning myself into a slave, wait until we get back home, then we will see who of us is truly a slave, some of you, or me."

I did not at all feel or think I was 'slaving'. In fact, I believed I was grabbing the opportunity in the land of plenty to enable me to change my profession from nurse to fashion designer and I was exhilarated. At home, in Zambia, I had reached a point where I saw nursing as a dead end. I found it boring, too much routine - get the report, wash the patients, give medication or dress wounds, doctor's round, tea break, repeat medication, write the report, year in and year out ...

Back home, once I had concluded that nursing was not for me, I began praying for the opportunity to travel out of Zambia again, so that I could seriously put my creative talents to use. I believed a bright future lay in changing my career to something I loved and enjoyed doing. Even at school, Art and Needlework were my strong subjects while Mathematics was a nightmare (which I even failed in Form Two, despite having credits and distinctions in other subjects). When I followed my husband to America, I believed God truly had answered my prayers, therefore I would not deliberately mess up a grand opportunity. I enjoyed my work at the Drug Rehabilitation Center; all I had to do was to give medication twice during my shift, the rest of the time I could work on my school assignments and creating my own designs.

I am not a routine person, I love exciting situations, and something new every single day peps me up. It is not in my nature to stick to the mundane of Monday to Friday, month after month, and dealing with the same issues bores me to death. Most of those embassy ladies were just typical housewives in the real sense. Even back home, in Zambia, they would probably continue being housewives, stuck in their comfort zone saying, "What will people say or think of me if I do this or that?"

In reality those women have nothing to offer, except being somebody's wife.

Dinner with the President of the Republic of Zambia, KK

One evening I asked my workmate to relieve me early because our President, Kenneth David Kaunda, came for the United Nations Assembly and had invited all Zambians living in New York City for dinner. One of the African American guards at work saw me in an evening outfit, and asked what the occasion was all about. I told him I was going for dinner with my President at the United Nations. On hearing the United Nations he flipped, saying something along the lines of: 'You having dinner with your President at the UN? I was born and live there near Rockefeller Centre, but I have never been inside, let alone been invited there for dinner, and you come all the way from Africa, you, your countrymen and your President are going to dine at the UN! I find this unfair and difficult to comprehend. Lady, the other day you told us you were trained in Germany and here I am born in New York City and will die in New York City. This means you Africans are more liberated than us black Americans, and this is not what we have been told about Africa and her people!'

I agreed that we are indeed more liberated, especially those countries like Zambia, which are independent. I told him that after getting our independence from Britain, our colonial master, the new Government of Zambia invested a lot in education. Citizens of Zambia were sent out to many different countries in the world so that they could be educated and develop our country. At the same time many friendly countries gave scholarships, in particular Russia, East Germany, Bulgaria, Yugoslavia, and many other socialist countries. That is how I came to be trained in Germany where I had a German scholarship. As for the visit to the UN, any person who so wishes is free to visit because the building belongs to all of us, the citizens of the world, all you need is a valid ID, I encouraged him.

When eventually the time came for me to bid farewell to my workmates as well as the guards at Sheridan House I remember one of the guards saying he felt sorry for my little son, because he is definitely going to miss ice cream in Zambia. When I tried to explain we had ice cream in Zambia too, he interjected, "What is the point, surely it would all melt?"

Can you imagine the level of ignorance? This was in 1971!

At the Height of the Cold War

In 1971, we packed our suitcases to return home to Zambia. Our plans were to visit our close friends in Europe before heading for Africa; in Scotland it was Dido Diseko, Abe's childhood friend from Lesotho. Then in London it was Anne and Peter Fraenkel, our mutual friends whom we'd met while in Zambia. In Nurnberg Germany we visited Manu, Abe's old friend of Asian origin from Zimbabwe and her Israeli husband, whom she met in Israel on a kibbutz.

Being already on German soil, I developed some nostalgia to visit one of my old schools in Quedlinburg, so I purchased a ticket and flew to Berlin where I was to apply for a permit to allow me visit East Germany. I must confess I was very naïve; here I was straight from J F Kennedy Airport, New York City, expecting to be welcomed to East Germany at the height of the Cold War between the West and East. After a lengthy interrogation, for them anybody from the United States of America was classified a SPY, obviously they had to deny me a visa.

I went back to the airline desk to change my flight back to Nurnberg. While in the powder room my two-and-a-half year old son was in the next toilet and rolled down the whole toilet paper. The attendant came in fuming and used very harsh language against my little boy, while shaking him vigorously. I came out, picked up and hugged my son, who was now crying uncontrollably. On my part I was already very angry with all Germans for denying me a visa, so all hell broke loose.

"Look at you, fat good for nothing illiterate toilet cleaner! I am sure you do not even have children of your own, because if you did you would have known how best to handle the situation in a motherly way. The child does not even know why you are shouting and shaking him" I exploded. "You should have controlled your child" she said.

"Nonsense, you are just a racist. If this child was white your reaction would have been very different."

PART FOUR

Back Home Again, 1971

Settling down when you do not have your own accommodation can be a real challenge, but thanks to Abe's foresight he had secured a job with the *Times of Zambia* before we left the USA, so we were accommodated in a company house. The security deposit I had left for myself and our son at the building society had gained some interest and that came in very handy as it got us a second-hand VW car which the *Times of Zambia* sold to Abe at staff price. Thank God the two most important needs, accommodation and transport were taken care of.

I was heavily pregnant with our second son, and my elder sister Dorothy came from Chipata where they were based as a family, to wait on me. She has always been a very loving and caring person, especially to me. One Saturday morning Abe woke up and said he was taking the car to the mechanic for a service, but he was gone the whole day. He came back home at 9 p.m. and I asked what had kept him so long – for an answer I received a beating; he was punching me all over, not even taking into account that I was highly pregnant. I was shocked, and could not believe what had taken place. This was the first time it had ever happened in our marriage. When all was over I said to him, "Next time and I mean *next time*, you touch or beat me, believe me, just consider yourself a DEAD MAN. I regard myself a very intelligent person and I believe in discussing issues not resolving them through punches."

He knew I meant every word I said so it never happened again in our thirty three years together until his demise. Abe did not stay long with the *Times of Zambia* but switched to a lecturing appointment at Evelyn Hone College, where we moved into a flat within the college grounds.

My First Visit to South Africa

In 1972, we travelled to South Africa with our sons, now aged two and four, for me to meet the Maine clan. What struck me was the warmth and the love with which I was welcomed into the family. The first thing that happened was for them to dress me up from head to toe as their *Makoti (bride)* number one. It was of great significance because Abe was their eldest son. His mother was in her sixties, very affectionate, caring and accommodating, I could not wish for a better mother-in-law. Abe had three siblings, two sisters and one brother. While in Petrus Steyn, Abe's home town, we visited his relatives and old friends in Bloemfontein.

In my absence Abe's friends asked, "Why do you let your wife drive?"

His answer was, "Why not?"

He explained that I already knew how to drive when he met me and I had my own car back home – how would he stop me! We planned to visit more relatives in Heilbronn but were delayed and could not proceed with the trip, so decided to spend the night in Johannesburg. This was at the height of apartheid and, guess what? Being a foreigner, they accepted that I could spend the night in a "white" hotel, black as I was, but not my husband because he was a South African citizen! They had to call the boss who authorized a waiver. Wasn't that crazy?

A similar incident was on our second trip to SA. We drove to the supermarket in my father-in-law's car with my sister-in-law, who on arrival at the supermarket said to me, "Sis we have to go this side and buy through the window."

She was young, just fourteen years old.

"Nnani my dear, go back and sit in the car," I commanded her then walked straight through the entrance for whites only, picked up a trolley, took my list from my handbag, and continued with my shopping.

Initially it was the blacks excitedly telling me in their local language to go to the window while I pretended not to understand what was being said as I continued with my selection. Then the whites started commenting in Afrikaans and I still continued with my shopping. I said to myself, 'If they want let them drag me out of the shop.'

When I was through, I took out a pocket calculator, summed up everything and gave the girl at the till the exact amount, put all my groceries in paper bags and walked out without uttering a single word. In the evening we had visitors from the Home Affairs Security department.

"Mee Maine, we are here because of what transpired this morning at the supermarket. The law in Republic of South Africa is that the whites and blacks do not use the same entrance, the door you used is for whites only and the blacks are served through the window."

"Ntate, thank you for the explanation, but I am sure you are aware that I am Zambian, not South African and that those laws are not for me but for you, the South African blacks. If I had to buy through the window, it would be an abomination, a big disfavour and a downplay of our hard-earned Zambian independence. Our president, Kaunda, fought tooth and nail to do away with such laws so why should I subject myself to that here?"

They got the message then started a chat with Abe in Sesotho. I overheard them say before they left, "Your wife is tough."

"What was going on in your mind? And how were you going to handle being kicked out if it came to that?" asked my niece Musonda when I narrated the incident to her.

I must say I was just pissed off with the apartheid laws; they simply did not make sense to a freed mind like mine. I was not ready to subject myself to such inhuman laws, coming from a proud and free Zambia, as our national anthem goes. In addition to that I went to school in Europe, I have travelled the world and as a family we had newly returned from the USA. What else could be greater than that? South Africa? No! While in these foreign countries we lived and mingled together in harmony with other nationalities - the apartheid laws can go to hell. There was no way they would kick Kaunda's daughter out on such flimsy reasons I convinced myself. The visit to South Africa certainly made me understand why my husband had relocated to Zambia.

Night Shift Nurse

After the birth of our second son I applied to Zambia Medical Aid in my nursing capacity, as a stepping stone to establishing myself as a fashion designer. I was in a hurry to start the business and needed to accumulate capital. Coming back home to empty coffers did not help matters and the only asset I had was my electric sewing machine, which I'd left in the custody of a family friend. This machine became the mother of *White Rose Limited*, which was to become a flourishing clothing company. My request to the Zambia Medical Aid management was to do only the night shift in order for me to do part-time fashion designing. My goal was to raise enough money to purchase two additional industrial machines and raw materials to set the ball rolling. The operation had to be self-financed because in those days, although there were generous grants for industrial start-ups, women were not eligible in their own right for loans. If they applied for one, their husbands had to be guarantors, which in most cases was futile - to sum it up it truly was a man's world.

This would be my last score as a nurse. There had been one patient with perforated ulcers who was of great concern to all of us, doctors and nurses on the ward. When Mr James was discharged, in appreciation he sent to all the dayshift members of staff a card, a medium-sized bouquet of flowers and a small tin of Mackintosh sweets. Addressed to me as nightshift staff, was a card, a large bouquet of flowers, a big tin of Mackintosh and an envelope addressed to Sister Katongo Maine with a cheque in it. A cheque continued to appear in my mailbox each Christmas for the next four years. This was the greatest gesture of appreciation I had ever received in my entire nursing career.

Someone asked what I thought made Mr James do that and my answer was he realized that my way of nursing him was different, with empathy and total care. During my training we were taught that with such patients anything can happen, therefore close observation should be of paramount importance and quite regular. I tiptoed into his room every fifteen minutes, the first three nights. Patients develop that extra sense to feel the emotions of the person taking care of them as we all become like babies, dependent and trusting, when we are sick.

It took me eight months to raise the required capital, then I finally resigned to become full time in my new career. I was never again to wear the nurse's white uniform.

My Entry into the Business World

In March 1972 I turned our spare bedroom into a sewing room and employed two tailors. I became established very fast, with a good steady clientele, but the bedroom could not accommodate more tailors, so we relocated downstairs to the sitting room. More machines were purchased and I increased the number of tailors to four. The clothes were designed, cut and made according to the silhouette of the customer as well as the fabric used. It was not 'one size fits all'. Women love this kind of personalized consideration, the sense of being the only one being looked after and, most of all, having that perfect fit.

There had never been a qualified fashion designer in our country's garment market, so the pressure to expand was unprecedented. Amongst my clients were Zambia's elite, the First Lady, ministers' wives, ministers' girlfriends, members of the Central Committee, politicians, women managers of parastatal companies and senior secretaries.

After a year in business cash constraints crept in and when I sat down to review my operations I found discrepancies relating to supply and demand. I was buying all materials and accessories and paying wages in cash, but was allowing my customers credit, breaking the chain. This was a gross anomaly, for a beginner. The amounts owed were staggering; a thousand times more than the cash the company held in the bank. That shook me and led me to take drastic measures. I changed the mode of payment from pay slow to cash on collection, or 50% deposit on order and 50% balance on collection.

There was resistance from some customers, but I put my foot down. Too many did not consider what I was doing to be a business, and my only source of income but a hobby. I told them that looking good comes with a price, especially if it is a professional involved in helping you look good. Another disturbing factor of working from home was the non-stop traffic of clients who came for their garments at awkward hours, meaning that our doorbell never stopped ringing. This became a considerable intrusion on our family life.

I learned that financial discipline is of paramount importance; initially it was difficult to separate what belonged to me and what belonged to the company. This was not just a matter of money for my own use but I extended loans to friends and relatives, who unfortunately did not see any good reason for paying back the money. Mr Townsend, my accountant had to put a stop to it. He said, "Mrs Maine, if you want to lose all these friends just continue loaning them money from the company because those who cannot pay will never be your friends again. Secondly, at the rate you are going the company will soon fold."

He came up with rules that would help me run the business within a framework, most importantly, that I must be on the payroll myself so that the temptation of dipping my hands in the company coffer was minimized. I heeded the accountant's advice and the business continued to grow fast and as a result more space was needed. I found a suitable place at Farmers' House on Cairo Road, where regular business hours would prevail, and my family would enjoy peace and privacy at home.

Move to the Farm

We wanted to buy our own place and to be free of dependence on housing provided as a condition of Abe's employment. It seemed sensible to invest in land. In 1975 before Abe's contract came to an end with Evelyn Hone College, we moved to the farm, a 25-acre plot on old Mumbwa Road (now Mungwi Road) that we purchased from Mr Rodger Mumbi, our brother. We spent all our savings building a three-bedroomed house, with no running water, no power, grey walls and we moved in. Thereafter we were stony broke and had to borrow K300.00 from Mum to pay the carpenter who did the roof. We dug a well, cemented around it and bought a Honda petrol water pump for the tank that fed both the house and the vegetable garden.

Out at the farm, our regular weekend visitors were our cousins the Luos. Martin had a habit of teasing Abe, and would say, "*Iwe* (you) Abe how dare you bring our sister to such a dreary place, with no lights and you leave town where comfort is galore!"

At the time my husband and I were thinking ten years ahead of our age-mates – owning 25 acres of land was an automatic plus to our name, as well as being the beginning of wealth creation, while our friends were content to be housed by their employers.

The house was a long term project; slowly we made improvements and added finishing touches. In 1978 we were connected to the national grid which at the time was very expensive; one bought the transformer but in essence the electricity company owned it 100% and were free to connect other homesteads from the same transformer without compensation, which I considered daylight robbery. Until we were connected we cooked on a gas stove, lit lanterns, kerosene lamps and candles. As for cooking, even today I continue to use gas; it cooks faster and is more economical than electricity.

One day in the late '80s, it dawned on our cousin Martin that farming was the future and the right way to live and he said, "Abe, now I see what you guys have been up to. The house is finished and you may as well think you are back in town. Please help me look for a farm or some land."

Abe did not have to look far because Mhende, Martin's workmate who lived in a government farmstead in the neighbourhood badly needed a house in town. Being an engineer at Zambia National Broadcasting Corporation he always knocked off at midnight. This being at the height of Zimbabwe's liberation struggle, Zambia faced attacks by Ian Smith's soldiers and Mhende's white wife was terrified of being at the farm alone with their little children. Abe put the two men in touch and they swapped homes.

Many *braii* (barbecue) parties were held at our farm or the Luo farm; it was more fun at the farm than in town. For security purposes we held parties from 6pm till dawn and only then people drove back to their homes, either dead drunk or dead tired, or both. Most of us ladies took no alcohol but were passionate dancers. One of my favourite activities apart from swimming is dancing. During the 1980s my business regularly required me to travel to the UK to purchase fabrics and I always brought back with me the dance music of the late fifties and the sixties when we were young, but the music we liked best was mostly from South Africa.

Martin ended up enjoying his farm and the farming activities. After his retirement he was always making improvements to the farm and enjoyed every bit of it. He was so grateful for the farm that he never stopped thanking Abe for helping him find it. May both of them rest in eternal peace.

Empowering the Indigenous

In the mid-1970s, the UNIP government made a deliberate move that helped to empower indigenous people to jump-start their frail companies. A parastatal company, National Import Export Corporation Services (NIECOS) was instrumental. To apply, all one needed was to be an indigenous Small Proprietor Company with a base of at least four sewing machines. There was no collateral required and one did not have to spend money up front, but one had to be prepared to pay Duty and Sales Tax as well as local transport on collection of goods from the airport. I benefited from this programme and my company expanded. I was indeed grateful to the UNIP government, for the wise decision to help small businesses grow.

Selling Fish, Kapenta and Caterpillars

To enable me raise the required money to grow my company I had to seek alternative sources of income so in 1976 I went in for dealing in fresh food. I would wake up at 4 a.m., drive to Nanga on the Kafue River, dressed in slacks and gumboots to buy fresh fish for sale. Gumboots were required because one had to meet the fisherman's boat halfway in the water. My transport was a Renault van which gave me an added advantage as I was always ahead of my competitors who used hired transport and had to wait for each other before hitting the road back to Lusaka. I would drive back to Lusaka to display my merchandise at any market by 8am, then by 10am at the latest I would be at Farmers' House dressed in an outfit befitting a fashion designer. I bought and sold fish five days a week for a month, after which I made an assessment about whether I was on course to meet my target sum; my conclusion was I needed a bigger and stronger cash injection if I was to meet the targeted time of ninety days.

My second action plan was to drive to Mpulungu on Lake Tanganyika to buy bags of dry *kapenta* (small fish). I was a lone female driver dressed in "hot pants" which were in fashion at the time. I had been driving for a long time, non-stop, when the car began to overheat in the middle of nowhere, and I did not feel comfortable stopping but by sheer coincidence there was a group of Italian road contractors nearby so I drew up close to their camp. When I stopped and opened the bonnet, there were wild whistles culminating in *'MAMA MIA!'* I checked for oil and water. They came closer and helped to establish the problem. They then had an opportunity to ask me questions, where I was going, what was the purpose of my trip and why was I alone?

"I see you have a ring. Where is your husband?" asked one Italian man.

The Zambian workers were equally surprised that I was a lone driver on such a long distance trip. This was viewed as very strange in the 1970s, but somehow did not appear so to me, all that was on my mind was to meet the ninety day deadline to raise capital.

Before I started off from Lusaka I was informed that caterpillars were in season in Mpika, so I would be able to buy some, and thereby increase my turnover. On arrival there I checked with the locals who said the chiefs had not done due diligence the traditional way, but that in Kasama the selling had started. According to our culture and tradition, for such natural God-given gifts as caterpillars, mushrooms and wild fruits, the chief of an area has to go through the 'Gratitude ceremony', praying to and appeasing the ancestors before the community begins to eat.

The next day I proceeded to Kasama, where I was a guest of the Chella family and made that a base for caterpillar buying and drying. To maximize my returns I was exchanging items such as sugar, bath soap, washing powder, salt, bread, and cooking oil for caterpillars, instead of cash. The buying and drying exercise took me ten days.

My Renault van could only take eight 90kg hessian sacks and I left it parked at the Chella home. In Mpulungu I bought *kapenta*, hired part of a truck then proceeded back to Lusaka via Kasama where I picked up my Renault and drove behind the truck all the way to Lusaka.

The caterpillars sold like hot cakes, while the many bags of *kapenta* sold more slowly but finished just a week before the arrival of the expected consignment of supplies for my business. I had raised enough to cover Duty and Sales Tax on the materials I needed, but was still short of transport cost from the airport to my home in Lusaka West. This shortfall was peanuts compared to the Duty and Sales Tax I had raised, but it still seemed astronomical.

The Arrival of the Consignment

I eventually approached a cousin, McPherson Mbulo, a major in the Zambian Army, for a loan. I first phoned him then went to his office. After making my reason for the visit known, typical of the joker he was, he made fun of me saying, "Is that the reason for this great flu!"

He put his hand in his breast pocket, pulled out a bundle of notes, counted K80 and handed me the money. May his soul rest in eternal peace. What a sigh of relief! I was very grateful and promised to pay back within a week.

I went to the airport and collected the goods which filled up the whole of our spare bedroom. I must say it was a large consignment. I could only thank the UNIP government for this great gesture to the indigenous and for their foresight. I engaged an accountant to cost the stock, whose total value was a staggering figure, giving me that feeling of being an instant millionaire.

When Eliza, my Kitwe Central Hospital former workmate got wind of my buying and selling different items, her comment was, "*Kwena imwe ba* Katongo, you really love money, for you everything is about money. You left nursing claiming the money was too little and now you have left sewing and are selling fish, caterpillars, kapenta and who knows what next!"

And just imagine, all this was being said in the presence of all my employees, just to humiliate me.

In response I said to her, "Do you know what? For me selling comes as the most honourable and natural thing to do. I live on the farm and currently there is plenty of green grass all over, if an opportunity of selling that green grass came my way, I would definitely not hesitate, but jump to the occasion. But you know one thing, I love and respect myself very much and I would never sell my body, which is what some of you believe in and would rather do."

"How can you say such things?" was her reaction.

After the costing of the imported fabrics the first thing I did was to find clients to buy and Safique-Kamwala purchased the bulk of it in cash. Out of that I paid off NIECOS and my cousin and from then on my mode of operating changed. I drastically reduced accepting customers' fabric for making up and instead encouraged them to choose fabrics from our stock. We also created our own designs so that clients could also select ready-made outfits. This strategy improved the cash flow by leaps and bounds.

White Rose Boutique

In January 1979 I moved from Farmers' House to the Christian Council of Zambia's 'Church House' on Cairo Road and established *White Rose Boutique*, which became well known across the country and in neighbouring countries for its unique wedding dresses, children's and ladies designs. We had clients from as far as Tanzania, Rwanda, Malawi and Congo DRC placing orders for wedding gowns, bridesmaids' and flower girls' dresses instead of flying to Europe to buy these.

At the time, one sure way of marketing oneself was to attend as many local and international (regional) shows and trade fairs as one possibly could. Fashion shows were another way we marketed *White Rose* products. These were staged mostly in conjunction with other special events in hotels and the *White Rose* trade mark went viral. After attending a few Ndola Trade Fairs, we became overwhelmed with orders from individuals as well as chain stores such as *ZCBC, OK Bazaars, Mwaiseni Stores* and privately owned shops such as *Les Petits Elegants* on Nkwazi Road in Lusaka.

Our boutique on Cairo Road was flourishing. At this point I set myself a very high goal that if by the age of forty years I do not make it as a millionaire (this was before hyperinflation) I should just forget about becoming one, but the business was so good that I actually made it four years earlier than that. At times we had to work even on Sundays to manage to fill our many orders. This was at a time when nothing was certain - sanctions triggered by Rhodesia's UDI were having a dire effect on Zambian commerce and the Selous Scouts were bombing and terrorizing our country because we supported and harboured the Zimbabwean freedom fighters.

During this period the Bank of Zambia began tightening the rules on the importation of raw materials as well as finished clothing as a way of conserving dwindling foreign exchange. The fledgling garment industry was hard hit because it was not regarded as a priority category. Three textile companies in the country produced a small range of fabrics for very limited applications, but the market had huge shortfalls of other types of fabrics, particularly the luxury fabrics we needed. Even big fabric importing shops such as *Modern Fabrics* and *Limbada* were affected and began to lack stock. *White Rose* was left with no option but to join the queue of importers to bring in specialized fabrics like chiffons, organza, satin and lace for wedding dresses and also accessories such as ribbons, flowers, threads, eyelets and various trimmings. Our fabric imports were all from UK and we got a foreign exchange allocation like any other manufacturing company from Bank of Zambia.

My Partner, Cathy Mwanamwambwa

I initially encountered Cathy Mwanamwambwa when her husband, Amusa, was the Zambian Press Attaché in New York. We met over a lunch but lost touch with each other only to meet once more in Lusaka at the Agriculture Showgrounds with our small children. We both were in clothing manufacturing in our individual companies, *Bimzi* and *White Rose* and we had the same strategy of marketing our products through trade fairs and shows. During one trip to London, when we went to buy raw materials for our individual manufacturing companies, Cathy told me that we had to be through with purchases by 16.00hrs because she had to attend a Christian Science Lecture at 17.00hrs somewhere on Oxford Street. I asked her what that was about and she explained that the Church of Christ, Scientist holds spiritual lectures to bless the community in various towns and countries all over the world. Having never heard of Christian Science I was curious and asked whether it was attendance by invitation and on hearing that it was a public lecture I decided to go along with her instead of our going back to the hotel in separate taxis.

While I was not clear on the terminology used throughout the session, I was sure that here was the teaching I had sought for so many years. What I picked out was the speaker's emphasis that God is love, that we are created in God's image and likeness, that we are his children and that God loves us unconditionally. And yet I had believed that God did not love me. I realised that I wanted to learn more about Christian Science. As we walked onto the street in search of a taxi, I said to my friend, "That was great, it has ignited my long sleeping feelings about my Maker-Creator and I am very grateful for the message. The speaker mentioned *Science and Health with Key to the Scriptures* by Mary Baker Eddy; where can I buy the book?"

We went to a Christian Science Reading Room where, as well as *Science and Health*, I bought my first ever BIBLE, (the King James Version), *Christian Science Bible Weekly Lesson*, some *Christian Science Sentinels, Christian Science Journals* and various other publications. That was the beginning of my spiritual journey. In the past I had rejected formal religion because so many things bothered me about it.

Back home I started attending a branch church in Lusaka. I read *Science and Health* from cover to cover several times in the quest to understand the religion. One Sunday morning as I was preparing to go to church my husband said he wanted to come with me and I said he was very much welcome. In later years his Testimony was: "I joined Christian Science on experiencing the wonderful transformation that transpired to my wife. Previously she was hot tempered, uncompromising and bridged no nonsense but now she exudes harmony and is very understanding. Out of curiosity I wanted to know what kind of a church it was that could change a person so drastically and positively the way my wife has turned out to be a perfect loving human being."

Saba-Saba Show

During this period in the mid-1980s most private sector companies were economically at the budding stage, while parastatal companies were massive and developed, but both faced the same major challenge – the lack of foreign exchange. This factor lead them all to operate below capacity. As the years went by we attended many trade fairs and shows within the region as one way of creating foreign exchange for individual companies and ultimately for the country. The Tanzanian *Saba-Saba* Show and the Luanda Show in Angola were particularly important to us. The first *Saba-Saba* Show we attended was an eye-opener for us to discover what was in demand or simply in short supply in that country; the list of what was needed was mind boggling, things that we took for granted in Zambia such as toothpaste, bath soap, toilet paper, female sanitary pads, vaseline, baby napkins, underpants, bras, lingerie, and shoes. Tanzania was going through the effects of the philosophy of *Chama Cha Mapinduzi* (The Party of the Revolution). Cathy and I saw an opportunity to rake in millions of Tanzanian shillings at the next year's *Saba-Saba* Show, so we planned and prepared well in advance. We flew to UK just before the opening of *Saba-Saba* Show and purchased good quality pants, bras and other lingerie, things that we could not cheaply source from Zambia. We declared them as goods in transit so that Import Duty and Sales Tax were not paid twice, in Zambia and in Tanzania.

When we displayed our merchandise the demand was unprecedented. Our two stands had meandering long queues. At the end of the first day we realised that more goods would be required so we consulted the customs officials to seek clarification on whether it was in order for us to bring in more goods and were assured we were still within the stipulated time limit. I flew back home to Lusaka in order to accompany a consignment back to Tanzania. On the ground back home we had very efficient employees and on my arrival I found the job already 90% done. The next day I flew back to Tanzania on Zambia Airways, our national airline.

I had never in my life handled so much money in a short spell of time; for five days Funny (my sales assistant) and I were just throwing money in a tin trunk and it was exactly the same for Cathy with Maggie, her sales assistant. Amongst the Zambian exhibitors there was one lady competitor, she went to the Show Society offices to lodge a complaint that we had brought in a second consignment. They told her to take her complaint to the Customs Office, who, of course, informed her it was perfectly in order. After getting that information she decided to do the same, (clearly thinking, "If you can't beat them, join them") flew back to Zambia and brought back similar goods. Unfortunately, she landed with her cargo the day after the Show Society's stipulated deadline and her goods were seized by the same Customs Office she had earlier reported us to. By the time she managed to have them cleared by paying a penalty fee, the show was over. I never found out what transpired thereafter – international marketing certainly isn't risk-free!

The money we'd taken at the show took us a full seven hours to count and bundle. The following day we delivered the two trunks of money to our High Commissioner and asked him to process it through the Central Bank of Tanzania and remit to Central Bank of Zambia as USD converted but our company credited with Zambian Kwacha. We had certainly made a killing!

Formation of *Whitbi Limited*

It was by now clearly written on the wall that any manufacturing business house that survived Zambia's foreign exchange crunch would have to earn their own foreign exchange in order to continue trading. After attending so many regional shows and fairs, my friend Cathy and I decided to merge our two companies *White Rose Limited* and *Bimzi Limited* to form *Whitbi Limited* with the single objective of handling the export market for the two parent companies. The reasons for merging were that we were competing against each other, except on the handbags my partner produced in her factory, and the wedding gowns which were *White Rose's* speciality. We decided that, 'Two heads are better than one.' The stake in *Whitbi Limited* was 50/50.

The turning point of our business – *The Luanda Exhibition*

We were constantly on the lookout for new opportunities, were willing to think laterally and venture outside our comfort zone. *Whitbi's* most significant and perhaps unlikely export order was from *Diamang*, an Angolan diamond mining company, for beef. It all started in 1986 with a small exhibition by a handful of Zambian private and parastatal companies in Luanda where we were to exhibit for a week. Three days down the line with the exhibition, the ministry concerned extended a blanket invitation to the exhibitors to a meeting, but specified that just four delegates would have to represent the majority because of limited space in their office. Everybody cried foul, afraid of what their bosses reaction would be if they were not selected, and we argued amongst ourselves for about an hour, after which our host came out of his office and said, "Ladies and Gentlemen I had hoped to talk to you within this past one hour, but now I have to go and attend to my next appointment, Zambia and Angola are sisters therefore our doors are open, once you decide on your four representatives."

Can you believe that? We never even got to know what the man wanted to discuss or had to offer! That was a terrible mistake, but typical Zambian attitude - *'If I can't have it, you can't have it either!'* This kind of attitude is not progressive and is one reason why, as Zambians, we have not made a big bang locally or internationally. We do not piggyback each other, we are happy when the other person is failing, then we wonder why it is that when poor foreigners come to Zambia, wearing flipflops, carrying only a plastic bag with one change of T-shirt, their compatriots piggyback them and within a short time they are wealthy. We then burn with envy and call them all sorts of names, like Satanists, or we begin to adore them, calling them "Ba boss", but we are jealous of our own and do not want to see them succeed if we ourselves cannot. Unfortunately, such attitudes are even found in families, sibling blocking sibling, even people who have made it themselves do not want others to do the same. This is a sickening and sad situation in our country, coupled with an 'each one for himself and God for us all' attitude.

There was no second chance given to exhibitors but one afternoon two ladies, officials from the Angolan Ministry of Trade Commerce and Industry, visited our stand and extended an invitation for dinner. Cathy and I welcomed the invitation and it was at this dinner that the beef inquiry was broached. The spokesperson (through Bupe Simbule, an interpreter working at the Zambian Embassy but married to an Angolan) told us that the clothing and handbags we had for sale were beautiful but Angola was at war. "We need food more than clothes. Our diamond mining company needs fresh beef, not the frozen meat we get from Brazil."

The next day all Zambian exhibitors had a farewell post-mortem meeting with our Ambassador about the Luanda Fair. Heinz, one of our fellow exhibitors representing *Serios International Zambia Limited* a manufacturer of men's suits and military uniforms said, "Mr Ambassador I would like to inform you that I am still with you for another week, because I have meetings lined up with the Ministry of Defence."

Everybody was happy for him, especially his fellow whites. All the whites who had some dollar change offloaded that on Heinz to help with accommodation costs for the extra week and wished him all the best.

At this point my partner also informed the Ambassador and the meeting that the two of us were staying to conclude some unfinished business. One man stood up puffed with the usual male chauvinism, laughed and sarcastically said "I can well understand when Heinz from *Serios International* says he is staying behind, but these two women what do they expect to achieve, that we all so far have failed to achieve? They should not forget they are married and their husbands are waiting for them back home."

My answer was, "Yes, the two women are married, but fortunately to very decent men who have high respect for them and are very supportive. At the same time, they are very much aware of all that is taking place in Luanda. The difference between you and the "two women" is that they are their own bosses, while you have to get permission whether to stay or to go home. We ask ourselves right here, now, and come up with a logical conclusion. Don't compare yourself to us!"

Back at the hotel, we sat on our beds, emptied both our purses in order to come up with a survival strategy from our remaining dollars. After paying for accommodation there was enough for only two good meals for the both of us so we decided to rely on a heavy breakfast which was included in the room rate (and took bread rolls to our room for later).

In the week that followed two very crucial meetings took place with the *Diamang Mine* buyers. When Thursday came we flew back home, both 2-3kgs lighter as a consequence of our starvation diet, but we had arranged to return bringing samples of fresh beef from Zambia. Being the *Whitbi* marketing person, I had to accompany choice beef cuts as samples in a cool box to Angola. Upon viewing the samples, the deal was sealed and a Letter of Credit opened for $1.8 million on Chase Manhattan Bank, USA for 30 tons of choice beef carcasses to be delivered by air freight from Zambia every Thursday. Soon we had a deal to supply the mine with beef. At that point my partner and I did not have a single four-legged cow between us, but we were confident that the order, whose magnitude was potentially infinite, would be fulfilled. Just how, we did not yet know!

On arrival back in Zambia with a confirmed order, my husband, being a journalist, knew major cattle farmers personally and made appointments for us to meet and discuss the Angolan business opportunity. We should have started with Mr Galaun at 11.00hrs, but he changed the appointment to 14.00hrs, so we went to *Lendor Burton*. (Mr Galaun never forgave us for working with Mr Burton, his arch-rival, rather than with him.)

After the introductions and the detailed explanation his question was, "Are you girls aware of the magnitude of this order and how many cattle will be required? My farm stock will be wiped out after only few deliveries. Angola is at war, and Savimbi will shoot down any cargo plane in the Angolan air space."

The Managing Director seemed adamant that it couldn't work but as his accountant, Paul Connolly, escorted us to the door his position was different and he said, "Ladies this is a fantastic opportunity for *Lendor* to earn some foreign exchange, I can assure you it is doable. I know my old man well, I will convince him. All we need is to step up the feedlot facility." He could not contain his excitement.

The following day, Paul called to say that we should meet *Lendor's* managing director once more. We went with our hearts in our mouths, not knowing what to expect. The accountant had for sure done his homework, the meeting was for us to plan and share responsibilities. *Lendor Burton's* role was to take care of operations, i.e. to buy cattle, apply for veterinary stock movement permits, feedlots, and take the animals to the *Cold Storage Board of Zambia* for slaughter. *Whitbi* expertise was to market, communicate with the client, arrange for export permits, aviation documentation, receive the crew and be at the airport to make sure the right quantity of carcasses were loaded on flights. Within *Whitbi* we split roles, my partner dealt with the *Cold Storage Board*, while I took charge of arrangements with the airport.

The biggest challenge we encountered was to find a freighter. We searched internationally, but to no avail – airlines were not prepared to risk being shot down by Savimbi. Our own Zambia National Air Charters gave us the same reason – though, the mine is closer to Lusaka than it is to Luanda, it was still a very high risk area.

An Appeal to the Head of State

The situation had become desperate, and we were fearful of losing the valuable order. We decided to approach the First Lady, Mama Betty Kaunda, so I called her Aide, Officer Mulenga to make an appointment for me, which she graciously did. It was easy for me to ask to see our National Mother at short notice as I used to be in and out of State House as the First Lady's fashion designer and I designed for her over a long period. The most significant occasions were when HRH Queen Elizabeth visited Zambia in 1979 and in 1985 when HRH the Queen Mother visited Zambia. Our First Lady looked magnificent at each occasion, in their company.

Upon my arrival at State House, the First Lady herself came to the visitors lounge and said: *"Naisa mayo impwishe ukwipika utumulembwe"* ("I will be with you just now as soon as I finish cooking my okra").

What humility! My assumption, and that of many Zambians had been that she just sat and called the shots, never lifting a finger to do such chores as cooking. When she settled down she asked, "Have you received the new stock of those beautiful fabric samples you showed me last time I came to *White Rose?*"

One rumour she was not aware of was that she actually owned *White Rose Boutique* and that I was just a front to her business because all items in the shop seemed imported and of such very high quality. These speculations were wild, especially since there was the 'Leadership Code' of 1974, which disbarred politicians in the One-Party State from involvement in business activities and as the wife to Number One, she certainly could not take any chances. Sometimes, she came to *White Rose Boutique* around 17.00hrs when the doors closed to the public and, ever ready to gossip, people who'd caught a glimpse of her through the window or seen her entering the shop out of hours would fabricate stories about her ownership. These would spread like wildfire – such things as that people saw her collect that day's takings. My nephew, Kalofya, who was a student at Evelyn Hone College, once told me a story about one of his classmates showing off the dress she had bought from *White Rose Boutique*. He'd complimented her then asked, "Do you know that the owner of *White Rose* is my Aunt, my mother's younger sister?"

The whole class laughed scornfully at him, some giving different names of ministers or prominent persons in society they thought to be owners and others saying, "That is Betty Kaunda's shop. Where can your Aunt or just any other ordinary Zambian find money to stock up the shop the way *White Rose Boutique* is stocked, to capacity! Your aunt is just a front for some big guys in power!"

One thing that many people found difficult to accept at that time was that a properly trained Zambian could perform just as well as foreigners, if not better. Behind *White Rose* was Selina Katongo Mulenga Maine, a Zambian who was trained in the USA as a fashion designer, a woman who understood both the Zambian market and global standards.

Anyway, the First Lady certainly knew who I was and I introduced the subject of my visit, "Ma'am I have come asking for help through you. My partner and I went to Angola on business and got a very big beef order from an Angolan Diamond company but there is no plane to deliver the merchandise. The Letter of Credit has been opened, with Standard Bank Zambia; the beef has been sourced, and it is for this reason that my partner and I are requesting to meet with His Excellency the President, to ask whether we can be assisted using a military plane."

For sure, it was a pretty big ask!

She chuckled and said, "To me it is like you are talking

Greek, my dear. The best is that you put all in writing because all this business of letter of credit and so on, is foreign language to me."

I thanked her and promised to deliver the letter later in the day.

Two days later we got a call from State House, this time from the office of Mr Dominic Mulaisho, economic advisor to the Republican President. The reply letter read: 'We regret that we cannot help because it will be a violation of our military plane flying in foreign airspace, especially now that Angola is at war.'

We were both at a loss and deflated, because we were confident the president would help, considering the amount of money involved, especially that Zambia was in dire need of foreign exchange. We saw the million dollars' order slip through our fingers but we hung on, believing that when God gives he gives a complete package. As Adam H. Dickey says in his article 'God's Law of Adjustment' (*The Christian Science Journal* January 1916) 'The fact is, all things are already in their rightful place, that no interference or lack of adjustment can really occur'.

We sent a telex message (in those days there was no email facility) to *Diamang* informing them of the dire turn of events and at the end of that same working day *Diamang* telexed back, coming up with what would be the end of the search for transportation and the beginning of the historical beef exports to Angola. The message read: 'We are prepared to use our Hercules C30, so please inquire on our behalf from the Zambian Aviation Authority what the landing, and other requirements, including the fuel costs are. You also have to quote us Free On Board, instead of Cost Insurance and Freight.'

What a great relief! We were very grateful to the Almighty God for this timely fulfilment.

The Hercules landed at Lusaka International Airport to lift the first ever export of beef to Angola. I felt favoured, blessed, honoured and in my seventh heaven, as I walked onto the tarmac to welcome the crew of the Hercules. The bouncing feeling was as though I was walking on the clouds. The instructions by the Zambia Aviation Authority were that as soon as the plane landed I was to go meet the crew, walk them to the Tower offices for them to sign the documents and walk them back to their aircraft cutting out immigration formalities. By the time we went back to the aircraft the *Lendor Burton* refrigerated truck was on the tarmac, ready to load the 30 tons of beef carcasses.

From the airport building, on the balcony many people watched the activities surrounding this majestic human creation, one of them being the then Zambian Ambassador to Angola, who recognized the registration as that of Angola and in inquiry asked, "That is an Angolan Diamond Company plane. What does it want here?"

A well-informed spectator explained it had come to collect a beef consignment belonging to Mrs Mwanamwambwa and Mrs Maine and this was just the first trip. The Ambassador was furious and demanded, "How can this be? I am in charge of Angola and I am not made aware of such a big and important thing?"

He also said a lot of unprintable things! At one time he was quoted as saying, "Exporting beef is not a child's game. They are just over-ambitious women."

We realized he was not at all with us or wishing us well – henceforth we just came into and went out of Angola without his knowledge. There was a lot of business overspill; many Angolan companies, embassies and liberation movements such as ANC of South Africa and SWAPO of Namibia approached us for supply of foodstuffs namely, beef, chickens, eggs, potatoes, cabbages, carrots, and oranges. For this we chartered our *National Air Charters* freighter carrying 38 tonnes, every fortnight from Lusaka direct to Luanda. This was the height of my business life and I was indeed busy.

As the profit came in from the exports I was busy buying properties, not allowing the money's value to depreciate through bank charges and inflation. The other reason was, Zambia being a police state it was not wise to keep huge amounts of kwacha in the bank, as that would just attract trumped-up and unnecessary problems for oneself. What helped us to increase the value of the dollar earned was the discounting of the 50% retention. *Whitbi Limited* being an active foreign exchange earner negotiated with Bank of Zambia (BOZ) for a percentage retention to enable us to use the same for our raw material importation for our manufacturing entities as well as other manufacturers. The central bank would pay us the 100% Kwacha but allow us to use 50% in dollar terms for our own operations. According to the BOZ records at that time January 1989 the rate was fluctuating between K10 to K18.49 to $1, the highest being K19.95 in December 1989.

During this same period, the UNIP government, encouraging the citizens to get back to the land, came up with an enticing economic declaration in 1988 that any manufacturing company that invested its profit into farming would be tax exempt. I purchased *White Rose Farm* which I developed into a ranch of 580 Buran and Brahman cattle within eighteen months. The same farm provided us with vegetables such as green beans, carrots, and cabbages for export to Angola which continued for another year, even after the *Diamang* beef order had ended. We also exported beef and vegetables in smaller quantities to Congo Brazzaville, Gabon, and Liberia, but due to the size of the orders we considered the business in that part of the continent not viable.

The first Letter of Credit was fulfilled and we flew to Angola to meet the buyers for us to negotiate for a second order. The Angolan buyers strictly work on commission and Zambia at the time did not have the word 'commission' in their vocabulary, as it was considered a 'bribe'. We asked the Bank of Zambia to see what legally could be done but it was a futile attempt. Zambia lost out on the foreign exchange from the readily available Zambian beef and Angola as a ready market, although the Angolans still wanted our beef, but only a commission would be considered. In this case the

Zambian bad law worked against the country it was meant to benefit.

We later learnt what had actually transpired during the meeting of all defence chiefs (generals) assigned to work out the possibility of the military plane involvement in the export of beef to Angola. Their whole strategy was to take away the order from us and let the generals as government wing handle the export. However one of the generals was of a different view and said, "Gentlemen, all of us here have our specialization, either we are flying, firing guns, arresting people or simply taking care of prisoners, but one thing we definitely are not is entrepreneurs; and that is precisely what the two ladies are, hence they were able to clinch this big order. The other thing is the source of beef, I don't believe we know where to start from, and whether the same *Lendor Burton* will be willing and agreeable to work with us from the Defence and not private sector. If we cannot help them with a freighter at least we should back off, and the most the *Bank of Zambia* can do is to stringently monitor the flow of the foreign exchange since we have reservations on that, though it is a Letter of Credit".

I am told their major concern was whether all the money would come to Zambia. They were suspicious because one of the partners in our company was a Nigerian married to a Zambian and the other a Zambian married to a South African, both of us having foreign connections. There was even some insinuation that we were being paid in kind with diamonds, so our activities and movements were constantly under the hawk's eye.

Business in a One Party State Set-up

I must make it very clear that politicians in the Kaunda era were strictly bound by the 'Leadership Code' which deterred them from actively being involved in business – it was the technocrats and vigilantes who perpetrated the nepotism and corruption. This point in itself draws the line of major difference between politicians during One-Party rule and the notorious politicians during the subsequent Multiparty rule who were involved in business, and were unashamedly corrupt.

Running a business in the one-party era had its own disadvantages, perhaps worse than corruption itself, because at least with corruption, you are a willing participant! (Not that I condone corruption; I loathe it) The Special Branch and the Special Investigations Team on Economy and Trade (SITET) instilled fear in the minds of the business community; business men and women were terrified, always looking over their shoulders as, it being a police state, the Special Branch were meddling in people's lives and affairs. The fear they planted was crippling.

Price control greatly contributed to the stagnation of the economy. Goods were sold at unrealistically low prices to satisfy the political whims of the UNIP government, and the price controllers were literally a nuisance, terrorizing shop owners and asking for favours. *White Rose Limited* was always under surveillance by the long arm of the Special Branch, especially as I was married to a foreigner who was also a journalist. As God may have it sent, I was not scared of them at all, because I had nothing to hide, and my personal principle has always been 'No bribe from me.' In their circles I was referred to as 'that rude and uncompromising woman.' In my operations I tried hard to stay strictly within the law, making it impossible for them to find any faults to pin me down, but it wasn't easy.

On one classic occasion three of them walked into the shop, and demanded to see the import permit and invoices on which the (purported) imported goods were cleared. I asked which imported goods they meant and spreading his right hand one replied, "All these in the window display and on the racks."

"But, Sirs, these are not imported." I responded.

"Of course they are!" he insisted.

Then I said, "Gentlemen, please come with me," and took

83

them into the storeroom where all the raw materials and accessories were stored. It had two levels with stairs to go up. I touched one roll of fabric and said, "That red suit you saw in the window came from this roll of material, which is also not imported, but local from Ndola Knitting."

I then gave more examples of things that were on display. I touched the roll of a lace material, and said, "The wedding gown you saw in the window came from this roll of fabric; this is imported and the documents are there for your perusal if you want." I continued the tour, "We are now in the factory, and I have twenty-five workers who make the so-called 'imported' garments."

I explained that the team they saw was behind all the creations in the shop: the cutters, machinists, pressers, button sewers, and finishers had all been trained right here. I explained that I did my Fashion Designers' course in New York City, USA and all that they saw was locally designed and made right here under my management and supervision.

"We did not even know that there was a factory behind here," commented one.

Another said, "Our boss sent us because he has had endless complaints from some of your competitors."

Such invasions were numerous and annoying, but there was nothing one could do.

One December school holiday, we were overwhelmed with orders. My eleven-year-old son Katyala, who was helping in the shop, came running to the factory to tell me a Mrs Patel, a client from *Les Petits Elegants* wanted to know when the delivery would take place. The order was far from ready and my son knew that fact. I said to him, tell Mrs Patel that we will deliver sometime today. He took a few steps to go out to pass the message to Mrs Patel but he u-turned and said "No I am not going to tell her lies, you go and do it yourself. You are the one who tells me never to lie and now you want me to start lying!"

He stormed out of the factory – imagine how I felt in the presence of my workers!

Kamra Shoe Factory

The export business was so profitable that it called for diversification and I ventured into shoe manufacturing in 1988. The clothing industry had become over-saturated and my interest in shoe manufacturing was aroused during one of the Italian Shoe and Industrial Fairs I attended in Milan, when I saw how easy it was to make high-heeled strap sandals using staples. When I came back home to Zambia I opened a Letter of Credit, using the foreign exchange from the beef and vegetable export. Production was simple as we used staples to make the sandals that went straight from production floor to client. Huuu! Was I not excited!

I called the new company 'KAMRA,' a combination of the three names of Katyala (our second son) Mulenga (my niece who lived with us) and Ralesite (our first son). I did not have to borrow in order to set up *Kamra*, it was all self-financed from *Whitbi Limited's* export proceeds. I appointed a manager, Mr Ketema, from Ethiopia, whose first responsibility was to fly to Italy with me to select shoe machinery for the factory, for proper mass and chain production. His second assignment was to train a Zambian and prepare him for entry into Cordwainers College in London.

On my way back from recruiting Mr Ketema a very frightening incident occurred on board the airplane. It was a Friday on a mid-morning flight, I was feeling great after a successful business trip, and was looking forward to being home with my family. I was proud of myself, as a young successful CEO, a mother and a wife. I took an aisle seat in a half empty First Class. It was a warm morning, most passengers took off their jackets and ties as they sat down to relax and enjoy the three hour flight from Nairobi to Lusaka. After barely forty minutes in the air the plane became extremely cold. Suddenly, we all were looking for something warm to put on; I grabbed my shawl to cover my shoulders, as the chill became unbearable. Then zoom! the door to the cockpit opened, and icy cold air filled the First Class cabin - I saw the pilot and beyond him a shattered wind-screen. My stomach sank, filled with fear.

The steward saw the fright in my eyes, came closer to me and whispered, "Please madam be calm and do not alarm the others, especially those in the economy class. Do not worry we are returning to Nairobi."

I had been on many flights around the world, but had never had such a frightening experience. I looked down through the window and saw Mount Kilimanjaro. Remembering that there was an international airport down there, I told the steward to tell the crew to land, but he explained that we could crash because there was still a lot of fuel, so it was best to fly back to Nairobi.

I was petrified and so were other passengers who had seen the shattered windscreen. Prior to the opening of the cockpit door I was reading my daily Bible Lesson. I tried to collect myself and recite the Lord's Prayer. Can you believe it? My mind was blank and could not remember a word! I would start; 'Our Father who art in heaven, hallowed be thy name' … blank, several times. Then I gave a soul request as follows: 'Father you have noticed that none of us your children is ready to go today, therefore protect and bless us all.' Having prayed that way, suddenly I was filled with an overwhelming sense of peace I could not describe and all the fear was gone. Then I continued to read my Bible Lesson normally. Someone noticed that I had the Holy Bible.

"My sister, can you lend me your Bible?" he inquired.

I handed it over to him and after barely one minute, he gave it back to me. Did he use it or it was just for the symbolic touch? On my right side was a young man, he seemed in his late thirties. He asked if I had a piece of plain paper on which to write a will. I gave him one from my briefcase. Before that, he decided to pour out a bit of his life story, how he'd just been promoted and this was his first time to fly first class; how his boss trusted him and he had a big company house, company car and a substantive living allowance. He also had a four-year-old very pretty and intelligent daughter called Mutinta and everything he had would go to her. He wrote the will on the A4 paper I gave him; he folded it and handed it over to me for onward delivery to his daughter - no address, no surname nor any other. He was clearly nervous and not thinking straight. Other first class passengers would come to me and ask, "Madam, do you think we will land safely?" Confidently I would say I was sure we were safe. When we landed at Nairobi's Jomo Kenyatta Airport the nameless young man came and claimed back his will.

While all this was happening one passenger was drunk and fast asleep at the back. I thought to myself, if the crash had happened he would have been the only one who would have had a good and peaceful exit from this planet. Up to today I have not understood why the young man believed if there was a crash, he would perish while I would survive and be able to deliver the will to his precious daughter, Mutinta. Secondly, why all other first class passengers thought I had the answers to the calamity we found ourselves in!

Kamra shoe factory came into being with a bang, the only competitor being BATA Zambia, a Czech company. The designs were of the latest fashion and high quality, to the extent that BATA Zambia placed standing orders for certain lines that were to be sold exclusively in their shops all over the country and this automatically tripled our turnover. Our marketing team spread their wings wide and found customers in every provincial town. Yet again it was thought *Kamra* was owned by a foreigner, not a Zambian woman.

Apart from leather, we used to import a twenty-foot containerload of other raw materials, mainly from Italy every ninety days, even small items such as shoe shanks, thread, glue, eyelets, resin soles. Later we approached *Zamcapital* a state security company to make us shoe shanks in their Luanshya Road factory. That helped tremendously to reduce our foreign exchange consumption.

The Foreign Exchange Crunch

Throughout the 1980s, Zambia had a strained relationship with the World Bank and IMF due to poor governance and poor economic indicators coupled with the low copper price on the international market. Shortages were rampant in all spheres of the economy; there were no medicines in hospitals, no essential goods like soaps and cooking oil – even bread became a product to be rationed and queued for. The government set up bakeries to make bread, scones and buns, but cakes were not included as they were considered a luxury. I remember one German visitor remarked that Zambia was the only country where the government was into baking bread, taking away business from entrepreneurs.

The business community was getting more and more frustrated, and distraught, and as a result many international companies had no option but to wind up, while the indigenous companies had nowhere to run to. They had to die slow and painful deaths, one after another.

The Solo Trip to the Seychelles

In the mid-1970s and the '80s there was a lot of money in circulation in Zambia, but there was no food to buy. There were queues all over for everything and anything; at times one would be in a queue for hours, just to discover at the end that you had no need for what was being sold or that the goods had all gone. Everyone was suffering from the strain of just trying to get by.

My husband and his partner were in the filming/media business as stringers, for *Visnews, AFP* and other foreign news companies. Zambia was at the centre of activities and a focus for Liberation news because our country was host to the ANC of South Africa, Nkomo's ZAPU, and Mugabe's ZANU parties of Southern Rhodesia, SWAPO of Namibia, Frelimo of Mozambique and MPLA, the Angolan political party. The rebel Rhodesian Army attacked and bombed Zambian bridges and other vital infrastructures indiscriminately.

In 1977 our marriage was in real turmoil, we did not fight physically but mentally and at the same time we were both trying to build our individual businesses. I reached a point where I was contemplating filing for a divorce and I asked myself this cardinal question, what will our two children's lives turn out to be from a broken home? My heart bled for them. I came from a poor home, but we were all together. Thinking of my children separated from either father or mother frightened me because it was unheard of in our family. In families where divorce had made inroads, it was said the children experienced hardship, especially if they acquired a step-parent.

Abe was saying he would take charge of the children, but would that be in their interest? I did not think so. But what really was the contentious issue? He was stingy and I mean 'stingy', and I did not want my only two boys to grow up with a 'lacking mind-set'. I could just imagine them as married men giving their wives the same raw deal their father was giving me. When he had to buy clothes for the children he would go to Kanjombe Stores, the cheapest shop in town and buy garments that might have one wash before they'd either shrink, fade or tear. I did not want to relive the poverty I'd known as a child, or for my children to go through that if their father took charge.

I could not make up my mind what I should do to change the situation at home so I decided to give myself a break to clear my thinking and I chose to go to the Seychelles. The main attraction for me was the water. I love swimming and find the sight of water soothing.

During this period the Bank of Zambia allowed only twenty pounds sterling in travel allowance. I asked my husband to request his partner/friend, who was an expatriate and had a UK account to send a certain amount of money to a resort hotel in the Seychelles for my holiday, and gave him the kwacha equivalent. I was in the Seychelles for fifteen days, seriously pondering the reasons why I was there. I asked myself the same question again and again. What really was the problem? It was not infidelity but stinginess. Could I change that? No, it was too late. Do I love him? Yes I do, with all my heart. Can I promise myself to ignore his stinginess, and continue with life as though he were the most generous man? 'Yes,' I said to myself, 'Katongo you can do that because the Lord God has really blessed you abundantly, in fact much more than he has blessed him, so you do not need his money to live well and be at peace with yourself.'

The evening of my departure from the Seychelles, I received a visitor to my room, someone I had been seeing around the lodge but never before talked to except to exchange a casual greeting. "Can I trust you?" he asked, looking straight into my eyes. He was of German origin and told me his girlfriend, a Seychellois, had travelled to Nairobi and needed more funds, saying he had checked the list of those travelling that night and felt he could trust only me. I assured him he could and he counted the money for her and gave me the Nairobi address where his girlfriend was staying.

Though it might sound strange, in the '70s there was no talk of money laundering (at least not in Zambia) so I accepted with a clear mind that I was helping another human being. This often happened in the 'third world' because of difficulties in legally transferring money from one country to another. On arrival at Jomo Kenyatta International Airport I took a taxi to the address of the hotel he'd given me instead of my earlier choice of booking, thinking it would be convenient. I went to my room and immediately called his girlfriend's room number. When I went to meet her I saw she was having great labour pains; she had gone to Nairobi to have an abortion. The nurse's instinct in me was ignited and I took charge until the foetus was expelled and she was calm. I then counted out the 3,000 deutschemark and made her sign for it. Suddenly she was in tears.

She told me she had to confess that when her boyfriend said he had given the money to the Zambian woman she was annoyed, believing that the money would never arrive, or be traced. "I am humbled to know that there are still honest people in this world," she said. She confided in me that the doctor had said, if she began to bleed she should go to the regular hospital for a 'D&C'. I booked a taxi to take us to the hospital where I waited for her until she came out of theatre. My transit stay in Nairobi was three days, and I had only $100 to my name, while carrying 3,000 deutschemark for an unknown person. As we went round the streets of Nairobi she said, "I want to get you something, so that you remember me each time when you see it." I chose a simple white and yellow gingham table cloth and now, four decades later, when I see it I recall the occasion and my three day transit in Nairobi.

You Must be a Nurse

I enjoyed every bit of my stay on those various Seychelles islands. Of significance was Bird Island. As the name suggests this is inhabited only by different species of birds. The connection from one island to another was either by air or water; on some islands no cars were allowed, bicycles were the only mode of transport.

I remember being on one of those islands. My intention was to see the giant tortoise and I had to hire a bicycle to do that. I had not ridden a bike for over twenty five years and wondered 'Will I make it?' Of course I did make it; after a bit of wobbling I became steady, and reached my destination. I was so relaxed that it was visible. A fellow passenger made a comment, he walked towards me and said; "You must be a nurse."

"Yes I am, but what makes you say so?" I asked.

"Well, we are at the same lodge, and I have been observing you as being independent, courageous and care-free! How do I know that? I live in a home with two nurses," he continued, pointing at his wife and his mother who were nearby. "Nurses are the only ones I know whose bravery is displayed on their faces; the same with you it is written all over you," he said.

The man was right – I remember one of those boat trips when the thought came, 'Hey KATONGO you are the only black person here, if anything happened you probably would be the last to be rescued, or not at all!'

Motherhood

I loved my two sons dearly, and equally, and was careful not to hurt my children's feelings the way our mother did. Even when I was pregnant I did not have a preference whether it would be a boy or girl; I thought whatever the Lord God gave me I would accept and care for, with all my love. The feeling of knowing that your own mother does not care a hoot about you is very painful.

The two boys were quite different from each other. The older one exuded health and was a happy, bubbly boy from birth; the younger one was sickly and cried a lot as a baby, but thereafter also enjoyed good health. I remember one incident when he was nine months old and became very sick and was hospitalized with diarrhoea and fever; he was teething as well. The doctor prescribed medication and a Darrow's drip but twenty-four hours later the prescribed medicine and drip had not been administered. Mothers were not allowed to remain by the bedside, they could only come during visiting hours and each time I visited I noted my baby's condition going from bad to worse. The mother's/ nurse's instinct was strong, that if nothing was done my son would die like so many others I had seen die in similar circumstances. I was determined that my baby would not be the next.

I demanded that my baby be discharged since no medication had been given from the time of admission and I believed I could take care of my son better at home. The nurses refused to discharge him. I became really wild and a nuisance. To try to buy peace they had to call in the doctor who, when he came, was intimidating, threatening me with legal action if my son died at home.

"Doctor, your threats are baseless, because in all this if my son dies I am the loser, not you, so give me the form to sign, and let me go," I demanded. It was by now about 21.00hrs.

I drove straight to my private doctor, a paediatrician. My request from her was Darrow's / Dextrose for me to administer at home and after checking on my baby she obliged because she was aware of my nursing background. At home I set up a drip and also gave him some sugar and salt fluid orally. I put a hot water bottle in his baby cot for warmth because he was stone cold. I was exhausted and could not keep my eyes open. Sitting on the chair next to his cot I dropped off to sleep but about sixty minutes later his cry woke me and when I looked at my son there was so much life in him. The ashen colour was gone, he was bright and he was warm – my son was alive again!

I loved outdoor life with my two boys. Either we were having a picnic or we were out for a swim or went for a movie. At times it was just the four of us, including Mulenga, my sister's daughter who lived with us; or we invited friends' children. Despite my very busy schedule I deliberately made time to be with my sons. Occasionally, as a family including my husband we would visit places like Kafue National Park for a weekend. I enjoyed the outings and also felt I owed my children that quality time of being together, especially when they were young. This is something that I picked up when I was in Germany where I admired seeing families doing things together. My favourite outing was *Munda Wanga Botanical Gardens* a little to the south of Lusaka. This seemed to give a complete package – a visit to the zoo, fishponds and simply beautiful botanical gardens, graced by two swimming pools - one for children and the other for adults.

I remember one incident when I saw a pig-like little animal running there, and I shouted out to my younger son, "Hey, look at the baby wild pig!"

My eight year old son coolly corrected me and said, "Mum that is not a pig but a warthog." After sight-seeing we would go for a swim then eat our packed lunch.

The last time we went together to *Munda Wanga* for swimming, an Asian girl sat next to me at the edge of the pool and asked, "Can we compete?"

I replied, "Yes sure, how many lengths?"

She suggested four. We jumped into the pool and swam four lengths and sat back at the edge of the pool again.

"Which school do you go to?" she asked.

I looked at her with a blank expression, hoping she would realize she was mistaken! She went on bubbling, "I go to Kabulonga Girls, what about you?"

I answered by pointing at my ten year old son. "You see that boy? That is my son."

She glanced at me once and responded, "Well in that case, you are the only old woman here."

Nonchalantly, she jumped back into the pool and swam away! She was right! Most women my age would never be seen in a swimming costume, but even when my children went away to boarding school I frequented the Ridgeway Hotel swimming pool.

They Left Home at Such a Tender Age

The boys' first primary school was Nkwazi and while there they both joined the judo club; the younger one had good reason for joining, because he used his skills to repel the bullies off his brother and himself.

One evening as we were having dinner, out of the blue Rali said, "Mum and Dad, all my friends have English names, I also want one."

"And what name do you have in mind?" I asked.

"John or David," came the reply.

"Well we believe 'Ralesite' to be the best name for you because it runs in the family from generation to generation and it has a meaning, while John and David, being English names as you call them, mean nothing to us," responded his father, closing the subject firmly.

They left home at a very tender age, just 10 and 12, to attend Bishop McKenzie International School in Malawi, a famous and good school where some Zambian parents sent their young children as boarders. The proximity as well as cultural similarities with Malawi made it most convenient, but after two academic years Malawi, like Zambia, abolished privately owned boarding schools.

One of our friends, a banker, had her son in Malta at a Catholic primary and secondary school which came very highly recommended for its good-quality education, so on one of my European business trips I included a fact-finding trip to Malta to view De La Salle College. Unfortunately, just one academic year down the line the Government of Malta turned the school into a day school. At this point my husband and I were now left with no option but to send them to the UK, though our plan had been to send them to UK schools much later, when they were a bit more mature, for fear of exposing them to destructive behaviour at that tender age. During this same period I had grown spiritually, and knew well that I was not actually the caretaker of our two lovely boys, but that God was their guardian twenty four hours a day, seven days a week, and 365 days a year.

At Framlingham College there was need for a UK-based guardian with whom they would stay during short school breaks. Our old friends Anne and Peter Fraenkel, whom we'd met when Peter worked for ZCCM as a young engineer and Anne taught English at Mindolo Ecumenical Centre in Kitwe, graciously welcomed them into their home. We set up some house rules for the boys:

1) When you run out of pocket money, never ask for money or anything from Anne or Peter. Call home and talk to us first.

2) Help wash dishes as you do here at home.

3) Keep your room always clean and tidy.

4) Always get permission if you have to go out and be specific with your whereabouts.

All this was said and done to instil some personal responsibility in our sons.

Anne and Peter are very nice people; when I began making regular business trips to UK they insisted I stay with them and not in the hotel. I had a permanent bedroom to myself where I left clothes suitable for European weather. I now planned my UK business trips to coincide, where possible, with the short school holidays – we used to spend good times together.

I had a ritual that as soon as I jetted into London I would go to a seafood restaurant, it was only then that I felt 'I have arrived'. It so happened that one time when I touched down the boys were spending a weekend with the Fraenkels, so I excitedly asked them to come with me to my usual seafood restaurant. To my shock they turned down the invitation in preference to McDonald's food. I tried to persuade them but to no avail. I for one would not be caught dead eating McDonald's food but I had no option other than to sit and watch them devour their favourites.

During school holidays at home in Zambia I made sure the boys learnt how to do some household chores. I was the only woman in the house, so we shared the cooking days – the house-help we had was just for cleaning the house, cooking was a responsibility for the four of us. If the food did not turn out good we all agreed not to complain but to advise how one could improve. Some male relatives complained that I was turning the boys into girls, but that was not the motive – all I was doing was preparing them for the future, because many young men of today do not marry, or they are lured into a wrong relationship just because the girl happens to be a good cook. The boys both completed their A levels at Framlingham; Rali, the older one came back home, did some accounting and joined me in the business; Katyala, the younger one proceeded to America for college education.

I Owned an Emerald Mine

In the mid-1980s, Zambia was in a frenzy of recouping financial resources from natural resources, in particular emeralds, amethyst, and aquamarine. My partner and I bought *G&G Mine* whose owners had no capacity to continue mining. Since our mine was next to the famous and prolific *Kagem Mine* we had no doubts about striking and all the geological survey reports pointed in that direction as well. We had the money and we invested heavily in various mining equipment on hire. We provided our workers with a vanette to go to buy fuel for the pumps and their food. We made our workers really comfortable to motivate them, housing them in a caravan which we specifically purchased for the mining project.

Initially both of us used to visit the site every weekend, then we began to alternate. One Saturday the pit had reached twenty five meters deep and it looked as if we would strike any moment. We drove back to the Edinburgh Hotel in Kitwe for an overnight stay, with the intention of spending Sunday morning at the mine, departing in the afternoon for Lusaka. On Saturday night a heavy downpour washed all the rubble that had been dug out back into the pit. On arrival at the site on Sunday my partner and I looked at each other in shock, amazement and dismay, we could not believe what we saw. I said to her, "Cathy, I give up."

"Me, too," was her response.

That was the last time we both went to *G&G Mine*. Our geological consultant and various other people tried to encourage us to invest further, but NO! NO! NO! Somebody asked a very pertinent question, "Why did you give up? Was it because of the money already spent? Or was it too demanding?"

"It simply was a matter of knowing the right time to call it 'quits'," I replied.

Interaction with other emerald miners made us understand the reality about the industry, and one important truth is that not every miner will make a killing out of mining.

Botswana - The Refrigerated Truck

In 1987 we left Lusaka for Gaborone on a market survey trip after hearing of a yawning market for vegetables and fruits in that country. Our first observation was how dry Botswana was, and that trying to grow any vegetable there would be a futile exercise. As we drove across the country all we could see were dry river beds, which was unusual for us coming from an area where small and big rivers had water flowing twelve months of the year.

In Gaborone shops, all we could see were fruits and vegetables from South Africa, so looking for a market was not difficult. We went to *Sefelano* a big buyer of such products and they asked us to provide samples, which we provided within seven days. A confirmed order was subsequently made for thirty five tonnes of assorted fruits and vegetables comprising cabbage, carrots, watermelons, bananas, potatoes, pineapples, tomatoes and pumpkins. The buyer's advice was to use a refrigerated truck for transportation of the produce.

We hired *Contract Haulage*, a parastatal company, and paid them up front. Before we reached Livingstone the truck driver informed us that the refrigerator had developed a problem so we asked him to open up to ascertain the extent of the damage, but he instead advised against it, because hot air from outside would make things worse. Livingstone being a provincial capital, *Contract Haulage* had offices and a workshop there, so the mechanic attended to the truck and we continued the trip to Gaborone, driving behind in our 4x4 vehicle.

We arrived at *Sefelano* grounds at 05.00hrs and asked the driver to park while we went to our hotel room to freshen up in readiness to meet the management at 08.00hrs to make the delivery and collect the payment check. The truck was directed to the off-loading bay. When the door was opened, we were greeted by steam and a putrid smell – every item was rotten.

"What a terrible loss, I have never experienced anything like this before," gasped the warehouse manager.

My partner and I stood there numb and speechless. There was nothing to salvage out of the thirty five tonnes of assorted produce. To make things worse the money we'd used to fulfil the order was an overdraft. But what had happened to cause such destruction? When we'd been to Chirundu banana plantations to purchase the nearly-ready green bananas we were advised to put ripener on them, but instead of working on the bananas exclusively, the chemical was inclusive!

There was no way to recover from this particular disaster but as entrepreneurs we moved on and thought of new ideas to continue in business, relying on our manufacturing companies. Later in my career, after a detour into politics, I was to see another dramatic loss when I ventured into maize marketing.

PART FIVE

Change of Political Wind

From One Party State to Multiparty Democracy

Some of the economic problems I have recounted can be laid at the door of the Zambian political system. Kenneth Kaunda is a Zambian born of Malawian parents who came as missionaries and settled in Zambia; from 1964, when he was elected president of Zambia as leader of UNIP, he made sure that absolute power was centralized in his hands. Due to his insatiable lust to remain in power at all costs in 1973 he changed the 1964 Constitution to establish a one party state. The UNIP government used emergency powers against the people of Zambia;, citizens were maligned, blacklisted and tortured, some even maimed.

Kaunda as a president of Zambia created a lot of enemies in almost every household among Zambians. For me it reached such a climax that when his picture appeared on TV I would temporarily switch off and only switch back on when I knew his speech or picture was over. I could not contain the anguish that the man caused all of us. No matter how hard one worked or planned, especially those of us in business, things just did not work out. I later discovered that the majority of Zambians felt the same way I did; it was not healthy for a nation to hate its Head of State with so much passion. We were sitting on a seething pot, which could explode at any time, and for sure it did explode sooner than expected.

Zambia had accumulated an $8 billion external debt by 1990. The fall in copper prices and high cost of fuel dating back to the 1970s contributed to the growing indebtedness, but the critical cause was that UNIP had the wrong priorities. The economy had gone to the dogs, there had been rampant inflation, the shops were empty, there were long queues everywhere, his 'Humanism' philosophy was the only thing thriving. Kaunda's priority was to share with your poor brother/sister, but what he did not realize was that there was nothing to share. The truth was that we were all poor and getting poorer every day and, as we all know, poverty can't be shared positively.

As a consequence of Humanism's emphasis on brother taking care of brother, most people chose to become too lazy to do anything tangible, but instead relied on handouts from relatives who had some substance and from international donors. The dependency syndrome became rooted in Zambian society and it has been impossible to eradicate, even now twenty six years after the demise of the One Party State and Humanism ideology.

By 1990 the country seriously lacked foreign exchange, hence one could not import even small things such as apples, cheese, biscuits, not to mention the non-existence of drugs in all hospitals across the country. Manufacturing companies such as Coca Cola, Lever Brothers, Dunlop, Johnson & Johnson and many others had to close. Other manufacturers had already packed their machinery and left Zambia to regroup either in Southern Rhodesia (Zimbabwe) or South Africa or went back to Europe. There was an attempt to replace the *Fanta* brand with what was called *Kwench / Tarino* – it tasted awful! As for household goods we had to settle for our local crudely-made items as importing them was banned.

The slogan 'GOD IN HEAVEN and KAUNDA ON EARTH' was perpetuated by all UNIP sycophants. Many Zambians had either to shut their mouths or face harassment from the Special Branch and vigilantes who were all over the scene. Being in Special Branch was a very lucrative job, and its members did not experience any of the shortages that we, the majority of Zambians, were going through. They lived lavish lives, drove expensive cars bought with taxpayer's money, they were hated by the down-trodden, hard-working Zambians. They were comfortable themselves, but were at the same time ruthless.

One Party state governance was truly draconian. It was alleged that out of every three people on the street one was Special Branch. No one could trust his or her sibling, child or best friend. At times people were locked up for fictitious reasons and seemed to have disappeared from the face of the earth. It was a real police state indeed, but patriotic and enlightened Zambians were quietly beginning to spread the message, person to person, office to office and house to house of what democracy was really all about, how other countries under democratic rule were different from ours, with abundance of everything and good economies. It was said that because of good governance they had decent hospitals, schools and high employment levels, things that had eluded UNIP's 'One Party Participatory Democracy'. The new doctrine spread like wildfire as due to the hardship the people faced it was easy to sway the masses from the One Party and Humanism ideology to a system of multiparty democracy.

It was no wonder that in 1990, for the first time in Zambia's political history, the business community came on board in large numbers to join the Movement for a Multiparty Democracy (MMD) party. Those who could not be there physically contributed heavily by partially or fully sponsoring one or two members of parliament to make sure that Kaunda went.

MMD Conceived

The architects of MMD were Mbita Chitala and Akashambatwa Mbikusita-Lewanika. I quote here from Mbita Chitala's book *Not yet Democracy*

> The occasion that gave me the idea for organizing an all-nation consultation convention occurred one day early 1990. While visiting Dante Saunders' house with a South African friend Latif Parker, Latif suggested the idea of holding a nation-wide conference to discuss the implication of Gorbachev's democracy reforms in the Soviet Union. This gave me the idea that such a conference could be held to discuss the inevitability of multiparty politics in Zambia.

My meeting with Latif was quite extraordinary. Latif, who was an anti-apartheid activist, had escaped from apartheid South Africa where he was a wanted man for his left-wing activities. He went to Zimbabwe where Edgar Tekere's Movement received and hosted him. Later, the Zimbabwean Government of Robert Mugabe deported him.

A Zimbabwean journalist friend, Peter Munyangangula from Mazoe, who heard of me in African political circles as a member and editor of the Journal of African Marxists, gave Latif my address.

With respect to the funding of MMD, the first money came from Akashambatwa Mbikusita-Lewanika and Mbita Chitala, which funded the first meeting at Garden House where MMD was born under the Chairmanship of Arthur Wina. The second funding came from individuals, of significance was the K30 million overdraft that Dean Mungomba provided the party from Capital Bank. Ephraim Chibwe as Chairman of fundraising opened various fund raising centers, including those led by Levy Mwanawasa and B Y Mwila based on the Copperbelt, while Dean and Ephraim fund raised in Lusaka. (Chitala, 2002, pp. 29-30)

The Birth of the Movement for Multiparty Democracy

One afternoon I received a large envelope from Vernon Johnson Mwaanga through Amusa Mwanamwambwa who said, "Read this at home. V J said you definitely will be interested."

When I reached home I quickly had my dinner and opened the envelope – I could not believe what I read, and that such a thing was happening in my own beloved country. Enclosed were minutes of six meetings that had taken place over the past few months – their content was to change the vision and direction of the nation. The attendance lists were mind-boggling, names that one did not expect to attend such meetings. I said to myself, 'This definitely is the second Cha-Cha-Cha. We have to liberate ourselves from the Kaunda yoke.' The tone of the minutes confirmed the degree of frustration, anxiety, and anger felt by the majority of Zambians. Enclosed also was a note inviting me to a meeting due to take place at Garden House Hotel the following day. The minutes rekindled and heightened my feelings towards the Kaunda regime. I had never before in my life time thought of myself as being part of any political dissention, but here I was ready to be part of this 'revolution'. I felt very strongly that because things were literally out of control, no patriotic Zambian could just sit back and fold their hands.

This brought memories to me of a time when President Kaunda had wanted to honour me as 'The Businesswoman of the year' and I politely declined the award. My point was that this was an award from an oppressive government, whose ideology I deeply despised. If I had accepted, what would that say about my principles? The evening before the Garden House conference took place I gathered my husband and our two sons together, and I said, "Guys, tomorrow I am going to attend a very important conference at Garden House on new Mumbwa Road, at this meeting only one of the two things will happen, either I will be back home with you, or they will take us to Chimbokaila Prison."

Our younger son was the first to react, "Mum what is wrong with you, why on earth would you deliberately attend such a dangerous conference knowing well you could end up in prison?"

My answer was, "Son, in each person's life comes a time when one has to do something out of norm for his or her mother country and the time has come for your mother to do just that."

The Garden House National Conference on the Multi-party Option was organized for 20th and 21st July, 1990 in Lusaka. At that conference a charter and framework of action, which created a National Interim Committee (NIC) for Multiparty Democracy was established to spearhead the campaign to return Zambia to multiparty politics. (Chitala, 2002, p. 21). According to Kaunda, we were just 'a bunch of small boys and girls.' Ironically, most people did not want to be openly associated with the meeting, taking into account the ruthlessness with which the Kaunda regime handled such matters. In fact, people such as Chiluba did not play any role in organization, so much that, even at the last hour he had to be persuaded by Newstead Zimba to attend the conference. It seemed that he grew cold feet. We were almost finishing the deliberations of the conference on the second day when he came and attended the last part of the conference.

The National Interim Committee was chaired by Arthur Wina, supported by prominent Zambians such as Vernon J. Mwaanga, Akashambatwa Mbikusita-Lewanika, F.T.J. Chiluba, Levy Mwanawasa, Ephraim Chibwe, Andrew Kashita, Kelly Walubita and Mbita Chitala. The NIC was a political pressure group demanding the end of the one-party state. A vigorous campaign of mass rallies that engulfed the country and the massive support the NIC received from the masses, forced Kaunda to cancel the proposed referendum on multiparty politics and agree to repeal Article 4 of the Republican Constitution, to allow for the formation of political parties straight away.

Initially he would say, "I am not worried about them. What can they do, the small boys and girls?"

He adamantly refused to consider us a threat of any degree to the continuity of his rule because he really believed the slogan 'Kaunda on earth and God in heaven.' As I said earlier, he created such a lot of enemies for himself that even members of his Special Branch never told him the

106

truth; all they said was what he wanted to hear.

Meanwhile under all this, the hot pot was brewing and boiling up like the lava of a long sleeping volcano, but Kaunda was oblivious, not even his Intelligence system got the full vibe, and the gravity of the truth that prevailed on the ground and thus he could not envisage any chance of our succeeding. The UNIP government used the Preservation of Public Security Act to effectively turn Zambia into a police state with impunity. This legislation presented one of the greatest problems to personal freedom of all Zambians. Kaunda had ruled us for over twenty seven years and seemingly had run out of new ideas. As citizens we were disillusioned, but those around him told him the opposite, saying that the Zambian people loved him as ruler in perpetuity.

One observation I made at the Garden House Conference was that there were only three women there, Edith Nawakwi, myself and another lady unknown to me. At this meeting a telex message from Sikota Wina and his wife Princess Nakatindi, who were in exile in London, was read out saying that they were with us in spirit.

During the meeting it was strongly felt that Arthur Wina should be requested to lead us in the interim and he accepted. However, during further deliberations, and at the Convention it was unanimously decided that Chiluba should be the one to stand against Kaunda. Arthur Wina was the better candidate of the two, but on the other hand there was a cloud over his head in that he had served in Kaunda's first Cabinet in 1964 and it was thought Kaunda would pull a fast one after the nomination and come up with a trump card of a skeleton in the cupboard over Arthur and cause his candidature to be nullified, allowing Kaunda to go unopposed. All these fears of the unknown were a reflection of how the citizenry viewed Kaunda as untouchable.

A second meeting was arranged, and the venue paid for at Moon City Club in Indeco House. Just when the hall was packed to capacity and the meeting about to be called to order, some Special Branch guy came and declared the meeting to be an unlawful assembly. The venue was changed to Akashambatwa's residence in Kalundu after some hours, so that we could prepare ourselves adequately with different clothes. We went to our homes and came back changed, men in track-suits and canvas shoes, pata-pata (flip-flops) or sandals; women dressed in track suits or two *chitenges* in the event we were sent to Chimbokaila Remand Prison. Tempers were so high that we were ready for any eventualities, come what may. The venue was not conducive for the meeting to prepare for the convention, however, it was noted that the afternoon assembly had some faces missing – those who were not ready to be Chimbokaila inmates stayed away.

Kaunda Repeals Article 4 of the Constitution

I remember the particular day on 17th December 1990, when we were in a meeting at the Ministry of Mines. One of our supporters outside the meeting phoned and asked to speak to Aaron Muyovwe, who came back and broke the great news to us that Kaunda had just repealed Article 4 of the Constitution. Aaron spread the news selectively and quietly, around the table, through short messages, to those of us who were part of the revolution. He dared not openly announce it, because most people around the table were either civil servants or from the intelligence wing. When the meeting ended we regrouped outside where we hugged each other for joy and celebrated the event. We now could legally operate as a party. The repeal had done away with the one party participatory democracy and brought in multiparty democracy. Someone commented that Kaunda did not realise what he had done to himself and he was now sitting on glowing coals! We all burst into joyful laughter. There were nationwide food riots, and Kaunda was pelted with tomatoes at a football match at Independence Stadium, something hitherto unheard of.

The Pope Square Rally

The first Movement for Multiparty Democracy (MMD) rally in Lusaka was held at Pope Square, where thousands of people gathered to attend the first ever multiparty opposition meeting. People not only came from Lusaka but far flung areas such as the Copperbelt. Representatives of the whole dissatisfied citizenry converged on Pope Square and it was unbelievable that people were not at all afraid of UNIP vigilantes and Special Branch, whose only known role was to intimidate and harass the masses. I am sure the Security wing was equally overwhelmed, as this magnitude of people was not expected.

The Pope Square rally ignited patriotism that had been smothered in most of us Zambians by the brainwashing through Humanism. Goodwill was alive again in all Zambians who felt downtrodden, and enslaved by Kaunda. Cash and cheques were thrown in a big carton placed on the platform for donations meant to jump-start the new party which was perceived as a saviour to all of us. The feeling was electric, our sole shared enemy being Kaunda and UNIP, all our energy was directed at seeing the Kaunda regime go as soon as possible.

Taking the MMD Dream to the Northern Province

After the MMD was registered as a party and following elections at the convention, eight of us, Michael Chilufya Sata, Ronald Penza, Dean Mungomba, Edith Nawakwi, Derrick Mbita Chitala, Robert Sichinga, S B Siame and myself used Ronald Penza's kombi to go and introduce MMD to our home areas, namely Mpika, Chinsali, Isoka, Mbala, Mpulungu, and Nakonde.

We were all novices where political rallies were concerned, a mixture of business executives and academics, except for Sata who was a seasoned politician and had been the District Governor of Lusaka and held a Minister

Without Portfolio position in Kaunda's cabinet before he resigned to join MMD. Our initial plan was to hold rallies in both Mpika and Chinsali on Saturday and it was felt that we should remain together and learn the ropes from the veteran politician, Sata, about promoting the new vision for our country to the people.

Sata spoke with authority, since he had been in this game from his youth in the early days of UNIP. The theme for the rally was *"Kaunda kuyabebele!"* ("Kaunda your time to go is NOW!") The emphasis of our message was on poverty and the suffering the masses were enduring throughout the country, due to shortages in every sphere of life caused by a one party state without any opposition. Schools as well as hospitals were in deplorable condition. These were hard facts, close to each person's heart.

The Chinsali meeting was very well attended by people from all walks of life: chiefs, civil servants and ordinary villagers. We were left with no doubts that the people were ready for change for our mother Zambia. The oppressed masses felt their saviour was at hand, and all they had to do was to rally behind that saviour. THE HOUR HAS COME! At this meeting I was introduced as contender for the Chinsali Constituency. We drove back to Lusaka, but as an aspiring candidate, I planned to return to Chinsali as soon as possible, to begin setting up relevant structures to facilitate the dissemination of information about the new party.

Tips and Training

Back in Lusaka we invited an American group to hold a workshop for us; mainly we had to familiarise ourselves with a lot of material about democracy. Zambia had been a one party state with socialist leanings for twenty seven years since independence, therefore the citizenry knew very little about democratic governance. It was imperative that our party members learn the difference between one party and multiparty governance.

"The Post" newspaper established

All stakeholders wanted to leave no stone unturned; they had to think of all means, loopholes and possibilities that UNIP might apply to retain their grip on the governance of the country. The major problem was that they would make sure that all the state media were instructed to black out any news about, and from, MMD. We needed a newspaper that would be in line with our vision, and *The Post* was born. The brains behind *The Post*, which started as a weekly tabloid, were Mike Hall, Fred M'membe and Masautso Phiri. The three approached and sold the idea to the business men and women who they knew were sympathetic to the cause of democracy and the new party and who also had the financial capacity to invest in *The Post* in order to disseminate information across the country. The first shareholders were: Simon Zukas, Ronald Penza, Arthur Wina, Enoch Kavindele, Theo Bull, myself, and some others. The editorial policy was made very clear to the shareholders, that there was to be no "sacred cow" when it came to reporting political news.

The 1991 Election Campaign

The adoption of candidates started from the office of Mr Emanuel Kasonde, the Provincial Chairman based in Kasama. I therefore had to undertake a trip to Kasama to deliver a letter of intent to him for consideration. He would then deliver it to the MMD NEC, for final adoption. Many years earlier I had travelled to our village Mwilwa, which is 110kms before the Chinsali Boma because I had lost my NRC. My brother, William Chitongo, was a political secretary in the UNIP party at the time so he suggested we drive to Chinsali Boma and get a replacement. That was my first time to visit the famous Chinsali, and I realised that there was nothing to sing home about! It was the lack of development that made me choose Chinsali constituency, as opposed to

Lusaka West where I have resided since 1975. I wanted to contribute to my home area.

Chinsali is the home and birthplace of Kaunda, and the incumbent member of parliament was his son, Dr Waza Kaunda. During the first meeting when I was introduced as contender for the Chinsali constituency most people felt I was out of my mind to even think I could put up a formidable battle against the two Goliaths, Waza Kaunda and his father, in this, their strongly entrenched home area – but it was my home too. Kaunda created such an aura of fear around himself that no one dared challenge him or his son. Of course I knew the gravity of the challenge I was facing but I was spiritually ready to face Waza.

My subsequent trip to Chinsali was the beginning of a serious campaign. I put my campaign team together, all through referrals, from interested stakeholders such as chiefs, headmen and teachers – all the influential groups of people who felt enslaved by Kaunda and his regime and were ready to support the new party. The warm reception we were accorded wherever we went by the local people was incredible, it just confirmed the fact that we were in this together – it was impossible to come across someone who did not feel oppressed by the current government.

We were well fed wherever we spent the night, so much so that Tembo, who had come to Northern Province for the first time, made this comment, "Mum, I did not know that the Bembas were such generous people. I cannot believe that wherever we have been, we find good food prepared for us and they don't even ask us to pay for it."

I replied, "Your observation is correct. In my opinion, in this country there are only two tribes that I consider very generous when it comes to food, the Tonga and the Bemba. When you visit a Tonga home, once the greeting formalities are over they offer you *cibwantu* or *musohia*. The Bemba will say 'When a visitor comes don't look at his face, look at his stomach,' meaning, cook for him or her. The reason is simple, these two peoples happen to have strong food security practices, so as far as they are concerned, food is for sharing."

There were four of us from Lusaka, Bertha M'tonga as my personal assistant, Shupa Njovu the driver, and Tembo my security man. On the ground Mr Chisanga from Mulilansolo Mission was very influential, fearless and enlightened. He was a retired miner from the Copperbelt and was an excellent organizer, having once been a strong trade union leader. He helped put together a reliable, loyal, committed and formidable campaign team.

Having grown up in Lusaka, I lacked deep familiarity with proper Bemba expressions. At times for lack of right vocabulary I would mix Bemba with English, and Mr Chisanga would note down my mistakes and go over the phrases and idioms with me after the meeting. Bemba is a very rich language and the right words and intonation have to be applied in their right context or the meaning is diluted, or even totally different. My slogan was: *'Umwanakashi butala'* (a woman is a granary.)

Unity of Purpose

Our first meeting was held at the Boma (District Government HQ) and this being a cosmopolitan area with a lot of civil servants from all over Zambia, we felt there was great resistance. Initially there were twenty five of us in the campaign team, including drummers and singers who composed songs befitting the occasion, moving from village to village. It was very touching. Everyone was a volunteer and they left everything in order to make it possible to unseat Kaunda, and be part of this great revolution - that was the feeling wherever MMD candidates went all over the country, except Eastern Province. The unity was as a result of the enslavement the people went through under the shackles of the Kaunda regime, but I believe the country will never experience such oneness of purpose again.

Meetings took place at schools and most teachers became our comrades, welcoming the new party wholeheartedly; they were truly involved, to the extent of housing me as their guest. However, there were some teachers who still believed UNIP would carry the day and were very antagonistic towards us. Children were used as couriers to take messages to their parents. The flow of information was high and this was to the advantage of the new party which did not have structures on the ground.

We completed the first round, touching every corner of Chinsali Constituency and were well received. The MMD seeds were sown wherever we held meetings and formed campaign committees, before we went back to Lusaka to replenish our coffers.

The Contentious Vice Presidency

During our trip back to Lusaka we touched on the subject of the anticipated government, in particular the office of the vice-president which was quite contentious prior to, and even after, the Convention. The party president's preference was Baldwin Nkumbula, but on the other hand our group of academicians and business community felt misrepresented, and our choice was Levy Mwanawasa. At one of our small group meetings, we foresaw a situation where, once Chiluba and his group were entrenched in power we could end up relegated to nothingness. As they say, actions speak louder than words. The old guard was not at all comfortable with the academics and members of the business community, Mbita Chitala and Akashambatwa Mbikusita Lewanika the engineers of MMD, included.

The group assigned me to invite Levy Mwanawasa to our next meeting at Dr Katele Kalumba's house, our regular meeting place. He attended, and was pleasantly surprised that there was a group that held the same vision as he did. After we laid our cards on the table he gladly offered himself for the position of vice president for the party and, ultimately, as republican vice president in government. At

114

the Convention, the campaign team included a lot of students from the University of Zambia (UNZA), and we banded together and campaigned so aggressively for Levy that he received a very high number of votes, much higher than the party presidential candidate actually got. Amongst us in the kombi was one who was against Levy's vice presidency who said threateningly, "Know what, we will make sure he does not smell the real power anticipated by you and him, of that I can assure you. Mark my word!"

"What kind of governance would that be if we had your preferred candidate and the president as the 'A' team? Don't you think it would be a weaker link than it is now?" I implored.

"Precisely. The point is to have both the head of state and his vice weak, so that the cabinet controls the government," he explained. He went on to say, "In fact it is you, Katongo, and your friends who messed up the plan and brought him in."

I personally did not see any logic in that.

Levy Mwanawasa was a brilliant lawyer, who as MMD party legal adviser, and Legal Committee Chairman, gave UNIP a run for their money. In the history of Zambian politics we had never previously realised that an injunction could be slapped on the mighty UNIP party and its government. Each time UNIP put blockages in MMD's way, in order to slow down its progress, which was furiously spreading and burning like wild fire, touching every point and corner of Zambia, Levy would take out an injunction against whatever move, and put UNIP's plans in disarray.

As the final desperate effort, UNIP came up with the notion of 'Heaven on earth'. Each province in Zambia was to have 1,000 young men engaged in practising transcendental meditation in the study of 'scientific knowledge of natural law' under the Maharishi Heaven on Earth. This was the last kick of a dying horse and a big joke. On TV we were being shown the images of people flying on carpets like sorcerers. Here I can simply say politicians never know or accept when the dancing music is over. In my opinion Kaunda's biggest mistake was that he overstayed in office. The same thing happened to F. T. J. Chiluba, when the electorate turned their backs on him. Every day at 17.00hrs cars on the streets of Lusaka were honking as a way of saying 'NO' to his third term bid.

In 2011, Rupiah Banda put up the most extravagant campaign Zambia had ever seen. His picture was even on lollipops for kids who are not at all voters. Despite all that he lost badly to Patriotic Front. I believe this mindset by the electorates will continue as long as we keep voting into office presidents who go to State House to line their pockets. Once this is established in the minds of Zambians without doubt then *'KUYA BEBELE'* (the time to go is up).

MMD as People's Choice

My third trip to Chinsali was to be the longest, most stressful and tiring. Exactly thirty eight days before the election date, I made Chinsali my permanent residence with my new-found nephew, Andrew Chimfwembe, a teacher at Mulakupikwa Primary school. I had never heard of him before, but when he read my CV he realized I was the great granddaughter of Chief Mulilabantu and he also was a great, great, grandson of Chief Mulilabantu.

Meanwhile, a lot had happened but Kaunda was still sure he would carry the day come the elections on 31st October, 1991. On 18th October Kaunda said, "I have never listened to so many lies and insults in all my life as I have listened to in the last two years. We have been forgiving them but after elections there will be no more forgiveness."

It was rumoured that Kaunda had pardoned 1,000 prisoners to make room in preparation for our imprisonment, once he bounced back to power: he would retaliate for the alleged derogatory campaign language the MMD campaigners were using all over the country. I denied that we resorted to derogatory language but asserted that Kaunda had not been exposed to hard factual campaign language directed at him in all the twenty seven years he had been in power. With no opposition parties, he had (no joking!) stood against a symbol of a hyaena, or a frog, used on the ballot paper to represent a negative vote – these never had to utter a word, no wonder our language seemed derogatory. Imagine how viciously we had to campaign to save our necks.

I had five vehicles of my own on the campaign trail. The bill for fuel, as well as feeding supporters, became colossal. I remember my younger son some years later asking this question, "Mum is it true that you were drawing money from your account like it was water from the tap, as my brother narrated?"

Three of the reasons why MMD believed I was the right candidate to challenge the President's son, Dr Waza Kaunda in his long standing constituency were, firstly, that I was financially able to handle the situation; secondly that no one could corrupt me and, finally, that coming from the business community I was not known in political circles and had no skeletons in the cupboard, making it difficult for my opponent to come up with anything to distract the voters.

The campaign was hot; MMD was seen as the people's choice but the Special Branch still told Kaunda lies. I remember one day, someone overhead the Special Branch officer on the so called 'hot-line' to KK say, "Your Excellency everything is going on well here in Chinsali. Dr Waza will retain his seat. All is under control. Katongo Mulenga is no match for Waza".

Quite contrary to that soothing statement, these were the most trying and difficult days for Waza, to the point that much of the time he was to be seen driving alone in his Land Cruiser, confirming rumours that he had differed with his supporters over the fact that they were not being truthful. He also suspected they were secretly campaigning for his opponent, which was not actually true. The situation was bad, to the point that even I felt for him, and prayed for him each morning during my Daily Bible Lesson. I would say,

"Lord, give the young man peace of mind to face and contain these trying moments."

In Lusaka the UNIP propaganda in the government-controlled daily papers was at its best, playing havoc with people's minds. One headline read: KATONGO MULENGA IS GONE INTO HIDING! 'She has been rejected by the people of Chinsali' wrote the paper. Seeing this, my family was worried; our son undertook an emergency trip to Chinsali, having told his father he was going to force his mum to abandon the campaign because she did not deserve the nonsense being circulated in Lusaka.

On arrival in Chinsali he went to someone he knew would definitely know our whereabouts. This person allayed his fear of his mum going into hiding and that instead she was doing very well and gave him directions where to find us. The beating of drums and the songs of a victorious team, the traditional ululating and jubilation, could be heard miles away. Our vehicle was covered in branches as a sign of victory and the songs were saying 'KAUNDA AND WAZA ARE DEAD AND BURIED NEVER TO RISE AGAIN. CHILUBA AND KATONGO ARE OUR LIBERATORS'.

I was the first to spot the vehicle my son was driving and, as I was not expecting him, his presence raised my concern. He parked, ran to the passengers' side of my transport and lovingly hugged me.

"Mum, I am here because in Lusaka the headlines are saying Katongo is losing and she has gone into hiding, so I have come to collect you, but here on the ground things seem different, tell me how is it going?" he asked breathlessly.

"Well, son, as you can see MMD is winning. If UNIP does not rig the ballot we are definitely winning. Chiluba and your mum are forming the first democratic government!"

On the stage during the rallies I was mostly talking about the MMD president, referred to as Moses, getting the Children of Israel from the bondage in Egypt, and leading them to the land of Canaan. Bertha, my personal assistant had to remind me that I was not saying much about myself, and what I intended to do for the electorate. She was a great and wise companion and may her soul rest in eternal peace.

Waza's Blatant Lies

Our campaign strategy changed, since this was now our last leg. We had to hold meetings in areas wherever Waza had his previous meeting, in order to undo whatever lies he may have told the people there. One of the cheap and blatant lies he told was that "Katongo does not originate from this district, she is South African, was born and bred in South Africa, her name is not Mulenga but Selina Maine."

My answer to all this was, "Sure, I am married to a South African, hence the name Maine, but does that change my birth place and origin? I have the midwife who delivered me right here in the district. I can even take you and show you where my umbilical cord was buried, but can my friend Waza prove his case in the same logical manner? No, he can't because he was born in the University Teaching Hospital in Lusaka, and his umbilical cord was burnt in the UTH incinerator. So who of the two is the child of this soil - Waza or Katongo?"

At times people would say to me, "What do you have for us? Waza has salaula (second-hand clothes), salt, maize meal and sugar for us."

"Well, Waza has been your MP for the past ten years. When last did you see him here to bring you all the things he has brought this time, and what development did he bring to improve the lives of the people who have elected him for ten years? Can, you show me any tangible project during his tenure of office?" I challenged.

"Never before – this is the first time he has brought us gifts and no development as you can see," they answered in unison.

"Indeed this is the first time because what he is doing is trying to buy your vote with the things you have listed. You will only see him again in five years' time during the next election campaign. But if you give me your free vote, morally I will 'owe you one' in return and will have to perform as payback. In any case all those things he is giving you were bought with your money as taxpayers. I do not have the money to bribe you, but what I am offering you is development, a better life for you and your children, good education, clean hospitals with enough drugs, improved levels of employment, not second-hand clothes and food that you eat today and tomorrow is finished. Above all I am helping you to liberate yourselves from the Kaunda regime's shackles, unless you tell me that you alone are not in bondage like the whole citizenry is."

Wherever we held meetings the attendance was overwhelming, so much so that those who were earlier shying away came out in the open to support THE HOUR HAS COME! Sometimes we would be driving through the village and on hearing the drums, the old and young would line up by the roadside to catch the glimpse of their MP-in-waiting. I remember a particular incident that happened right in the interior of Chinsali, in Chief Mubanga's chiefdom. An extremely healthy looking, beautiful, wrinkled old woman, seemingly in her nineties walked towards me, warmly hugged me and said, "My child Katongo, I am glad you are here. I have been waiting for you to come so that I can ask you this question. Are you sure this man Kaunda will not kill all of us when we vote for you and Chiluba and not for him and Waza his son?"

I was touched and humbled and said to her, "Mum you do not have to fear or worry because your vote is only known to you; those telling you otherwise are just scaring you."

Her shoulders dropped, you could see she felt such a relief and was at peace with herself and her choice of candidate.

The Final Touch

One of the techniques we were taught was to first handle the "pro-you" areas, making sure they are all on our side, then at

120

the end deal with the areas that we viewed as problematic during earlier visits. Chinsali Boma was indeed a thorn in the flesh, but we were ready to confront any challenges that lay ahead of us. The first stumbling block was the Police Station. When I sent Mr Chisanga to collect the permit for our last rally before the election day, he came back empty handed and said they said we could not have the meeting because Waza was also to have his last meeting here. Fuming I personally went there and confronted Officer Mwila, asking him to give me one very good reason why Waza should now be the law.

"I have followed the stipulated law to the letter," I said. "The permit was applied for three weeks ago and at that time there was no mention of Waza's request. You know what, Officer, you are so blind you cannot see that when the votes are counted and done with, Chiluba will be the Republican President, not Kaunda, and this Katongo (pointing at myself) will be the MP for Chinsali Constituency, not Waza. Officer Mwila, I promise you this - on my next trip to Chinsali you will be saluting me as your member of parliament as well as government official. But you know what? You can keep your permit. But the meeting goes on, as planned, and if you attempt to stop the meeting, be ready for the consequence and the rage from the multitude of people you have seen. By the way, how many of your officers are at the Station – four, five, or seven? By the time you get help from far-flung areas there will only be rubble to tell the story of an Officer Mwila who could not read what was clearly written on the wall."

I was wild, angry, and stormed out of the police station with my group of supporters.

The meeting started, but my height meant that few could see me because most people were standing, so I requested the table from a nearby house to stand on so I could be seen by everyone. I addressed the crowd along these lines, "This is our last rally and I am sure we will all vote wisely tomorrow, in order to free ourselves from the yoke and shackles of the Kaunda regime. I stand here mainly to thank you for the votes you will give to our President Chiluba the MOSES OF OUR TIME, and the votes you will give to me tomorrow as your Member of Parliament. *UMWANAKASHI BUTALA!*

"*MWIKALABA, MAILO MULI NOKUBIKA ITONI PA NKOLOKO.* (Do not forget to put a mark on the clock tomorrow.) I am grateful that I came knowing no single soul in Chinsali but now I belong to a big family, but since MMD is winning tomorrow, you will see more and more of me in the near future for us to plan and bring development to our impoverished Chinsali Constituency."

In the morning, while the voting was going on I inquired from the presiding officer how many vehicles were assigned to collect ballot boxes, and where the starting points would be. My plan was to assign a vehicle to follow each truck carrying ballot boxes, taking no chances in case UNIP decided to be desperate enough to start stuffing the ballot boxes with marked papers halfway to the counting centre. Not knowing the distance we fuelled the two vehicles full tank and carried extra fuel in some jerry cans.

We had to bring 3 x 200 litre drums of fuel from Lusaka because in Chinsali, as in the rest of the country, there was a shortage of fuel. The instructions were to follow the truck, if it stops, you also stop. One driver reported being threatened and told off, but having come from Lusaka he was enlightened and brave enough to answer back that he was following his boss' instructions.

The Day of Reckoning

The counting took place at Chinsali Girls' Secondary School, and started at 18.00hrs. I had never in my lifetime voted, nor been in a place where votes were counted. My reason for not taking part in voting in the past was simply because Kaunda was the only human contender for close to three decades, standing either against a frog, a hyaena, or a crocodile. There was no rule to force people to vote. I believe Kaunda was in his comfort zone, knowing that not many people would be that crazy as to vote for a frog or hyaena even if they opposed him!

When the counting started I saw that there were four trays on the table, one for Kaunda, one for Waza, one for Chiluba and one for Katongo. The bundles going into Chiluba and Katongo's trays were more than those placed in Kaunda's and Waza's. Not being certain I turned to Mr Chisanga who was standing behind me and asked what those clips of papers meant?

"Mama, they are one hundred each, it means you and Chiluba are leading".

All this time Waza was absent. He walked in when the counting was on ballot box number seven. He stood next to me, whispered to his representative on his right side asking, "What is the situation like?"

"It is pretty bad. MMD is leading with both candidates," the man said.

The counting continued still with MMD leading. There were some polling stations where both Kaunda and Waza would get a paltry three votes or zero; the people had spoken! The ballot box from Mundu was counted and Waza loudly protested that, *"Ine teti nduse pa Mundu"* (No way can I lose at Mundu).

We all wondered why Mundu in particular. Waza became unruly until the police officer had to threaten him with ejection from the polling station.

All MMD Representatives Turned on their Torches

Around 21.00hrs the expected happened, ZESCO power went off. We were in total darkness, but I had instructed my son to park the car strategically at the entrance to the hall and gave instructions never at all to doze, not even for a second, and when the lights go off he should switch on the car lights full blast. That is exactly what happened. In a split second the hall was fully lit; in addition, all MMD representatives turned on their torches which I had bought in anticipation of such tricks. Everybody was surprised but stood still. All this was due to our suspicion that UNIP would not sit idle while their boat was sinking and that while the power was off the rigging would take place. There were murmurs from UNIP representatives, one was overheard saying, "This woman, what on earth will she not think of!"

It took longer for the counting of votes in Chinsali than elsewhere in the whole of Zambia, so much so that people in Lusaka lost hope of MMD's victory in Chinsali, taking into account the wild propaganda that had preceded the elections, portraying Waza as the winner. But the time of reckoning had come. At 06.00hrs the presiding officer announced the winner: Katongo Mulenga. I was lifted shoulder high, there was so much joy and celebrating for all involved. This time I bent my own rule of 'no money for alcohol' and gave Mr Chisanga cash to buy as much beer as he possibly could for the organizers and voters to drink their heads off. We got into vehicles en route for Lusaka, an 800 kilometre journey. I was indeed grateful and happy for the landslide victory over Dr Waza Kaunda! It was a mammoth battle for me, fighting the two Goliaths, the father and the son. I knew MMD would ultimately emerge the winner, but at the back of my mind I suspected UNIP being capable of rigging, and what if they did?

PART SIX

The MMD Party Forms the Third Republican Government

It was unbelievable. There was delicious victory in the air for MMD all over the country and Zambians celebrated like no man's business. The strong man, Kenneth David Kaunda was whacked, peacefully, by the so called 'small girls and boys'! There was confusion in UNIP circles, because everything had happened so fast and the loss on their part was totally unexpected. We were told that Kaunda had deliberately made the campaign period short so that the MMD party would be caught napping.

They took advantage of the vastness of the country, and that the party was new to most Zambians, but UNIP ended up shocking themselves. The people of Zambia had spoken. Kaunda could not believe the state of results, neither did we, as victors – the margins seemed too high, but one thing he must have learnt from this event was that his intelligence officers had often lied to him. MMD swept seats over the whole country, except Eastern Province which remained a UNIP stronghold. For the first time in close to three decades there was an opposition party, not only in parliament, but also in government. MMD was represented by 125 parliamentarians against twenty five UNIP parliamentarians. Chiluba's vote was 972,212 (75.76%), and Kenneth Kaunda's was 311,022 (24.24%). Kaunda could not believe it and he accused the MMD, together with the Americans, of having rigged the elections, but the elections were declared free and fair by all monitors –the local ones as well as those of the Jimmy Carter Foundation. Kaunda was magnanimous in defeat, in a statesmanlike manner he conceded and handed over power to Chiluba with no resistance. I give him credit for that.

Chiluba Forms his First Cabinet

After being sworn in, Chiluba's first responsibility was to put together his cabinet. Some MPs craved jobs more than others, and not being sure of whether Chiluba would give them cabinet jobs, they decided to camp at Chiluba's temporary residence, living on buns and bottles of Fanta or Coke purchased from the bicycle vendors. They only went home for a shower before returning to camp. They told Chiluba they would not move until they were assured of cabinet jobs. Only with such resilience did they get what they wanted. I kept away and did not ask for any position in the cabinet because my plans were to remain a backbencher, continuing to run my business while helping to develop the underdeveloped Chinsali constituency, as these two matters were of prime importance to me.

For the first time in the history of Zambian politics there were many MPs who were professionals, with doctorates in various fields, but Chiluba made them all deputy ministers, except for Dr Kawimbe, who was given a cabinet portfolio in the Ministry of Health. Why? Because Chiluba resented and despised intellectuals, including the two who risked, planned, and used their resources, to come up with the formation of MMD. He was on many occasions quoted as saying, *"Tulemona, inga balelya ama degrees"* (We will see if they can eat their degrees.) That is how spiteful he was.

The Cabinet

The Cabinet included Levy Mwanawasa as Vice President, Emanuel Kasonde as Minister of Finance, B.Y. Mwila at Defence, R.D.S. Penza at Industry, Arthur Wina at Education, Michael Sata at Local Government, Humphrey Mulemba at Mines, Guy Scott at Agriculture, Baldwin Nkumbula at Youth and Sport, E. C. Chibwe at Works and Supply, Andrew Kashita at Transport and Communications, V.J. Mwaanga at Foreign Affairs, Dr. R. Chongwe, at Legal Affairs, Dr B. Kawimbe at Health, Dr. L. Sondashi at Labour, Gen. Christon Tembo at Tourism, Gen. Miyanda as Minister Without Portfolio, and at Home Affairs was Newstead Zimba. At Information was Stan Kristafor, at Lands there was Dawson Lupunga, at Energy and Water was Alfeyo Hambayi, Technical Education was Akashambatwa Lewanika. The deputies to the ministers were: Mbita Chitala at Finance, Dr. C. Kalima at Agriculture, Dean Mungomba at Planning, Deepak Patel at Industry, Dr. Machungwa at Labour, Dr. Katele Kalumba at Health, Katongo Maine at Youth and Sport, Nakatindi Wina at Social Welfare, Col. Chanda Sosala at Home Affairs, Edith Nawakwi at Energy and Water, Amusa Mwanamwambwa at Tourism, Dr. Mathias Mpande at Mines and many more.

I was at first shocked and then angered that Chiluba had denied us a single female Cabinet Minister! Women were given Deputy Minister Portfolios as follows, as we have seen: Edith Nawakwi at Energy; Katongo Maine at Youth, Sport and Child Development, and Nakatindi Wina at the Ministry of Social Welfare. Other prominent women such as Dr. Inonge Mbikusita-Lewanika, and Chilufya Kapwepwe were left out completely.

After the swearing in ceremony at State House, within the State House grounds I saw V.J. Mwaanga going to the carpark and beckoned to him and said, "V.J., you and your fellow male chauvinist pigs, why have you denied us even just one female in the Cabinet, what is it that you men can do which we as women are unable to do? For example take Inonge, with her doctorate she already has achieved more than all of you men put together, but you still have denied her even the lousy Deputy Portfolio! Why?"

"Katongo, I was not even part of the selection team," he said.

His answer shook me; that meant MMD powers were hijacked from day one. I expected people like V.J. Mwaanga to be part of the selection team, and eventually, part of the 'Kitchen government', because he was partly instrumental in organizing the Garden House Conference, he, Mbita Chitala, and Akashambatwa Mbikusita Lewanika. The Chilubas, the Sampas and the Newstead Zimbas came in later.

I did not accept the job I was offered. I told those close to me that I was not going to take up the post, let him give it to those who want jobs because it will interfere with running my businesses. I was advised to take it up and then later, in a cordial manner, tender my resignation. It took me two weeks to come to terms with this interference then I resumed work at the Ministry of Youth Sport and Child Development with Baldwin Nkumbula as my boss. He had a good personality and respect for age and we worked as a team. We discussed matters of the Ministry together before they were dealt with. I was more on the ground than he was, at times he would be very far away and then realize he had someone coming to his office for a meeting. He would call and say, "Mrs Maine, please attend to so and so, in my office, and the subject is such and such." After the discussion, if a letter was required I would dictate to his secretary and wait for his signature when he came to the office.

Once he instructed his secretary in my presence, saying, "Please give the Cabinet Minutes to Mrs Maine to read each time I bring them, because we have come a long way together in fighting for change."

I was grateful, because my fellow Deputy Ministers were agonizing with their bosses and I am told at times they were not even on speaking terms. They were ignored and made to feel they were not part of the Ministry, you can imagine how they felt! In fact Chiluba liked that, because his style of leadership was simple – DIVIDE AND RULE.

First SOS Children's Village Established in Zambia

Coming from the business world, time keeping was of paramount importance to me. My daily programme of duties was tight. Normally I was at the Ministry at 07.30hrs and dealt with what I considered urgent for the day, and by 09.15hrs I left the office for Parliament for the next eight hours. I also had to travel abroad – one trip took me to the Maldives for a Commonwealth Sports Ministers' annual meeting and another to Tunisia for the Africa Sports Ministers' meeting.

In my short lived tenure of office at the Ministry, Baldwin Nkumbula gave me a lot of chances to serve Mother Zambia in many ways, locally and internationally. One significant trip took me to South Africa to acquaint ourselves as a government with the ideology behind the SOS CHILDREN'S VILLAGES that are dotted around the world. Just for the record, the UNIP government was once approached by the organisation but turned down the offer because according to HUMANISM orphans had to be looked after by the family and not orphanages.

However, on my return I gave a report which led to the setting up of the first ever SOS Children's Village in Zambia, in Lusaka, on the Great North Road. MMD as a government found the offer irresistible, because as a policy the SOS does not require any input from the host country apart from free land on which to build the Children's Village. They also do not condone interference in the running of the institution by the host country. The MMD government's policy towards orphans was different from that of the former UNIP government because by 1990 as a country we were inundated with more orphans on the streets than during the Humanism era fifteen years earlier, due to the HIV pandemic.

A Heavy Workload

Holding a ministerial portfolio and wearing a hat as member of parliament does not give one much time to run a business, even to supervise by remote control becomes impossible. There were times when the *Kamra Production* manager would badly need administrative input from me but I would be occupied either with ministerial or legislative commitments. This pattern of work continued to such an extent that, sadly, my business was no longer my priority but came third on my list, with the result that when Mr Ketema's contract came to an end he got himself a job with *BATA* Canada. As though this was not enough to destabilize the company, the flow of raw materials was now erratic and became a fraction of what we used to bring in for two reasons: firstly the *Kamra* Company was cash strapped after

I had spent so much on the political campaign and secondly, the country had reached its lowest levels of foreign exchange reserves. Where we used to buy a container-load of supplies, now we could only bring in one or two pallets.

I kept my campaign promise and used to visit the constituency every month because Chinsali was the least developed district in the Northern Province, despite having produced a large number of influential politicians who were freedom fighters with high portfolios in the UNIP government. I wanted to see the place transformed.

My salary as a deputy minister was K5,350.00. This barely took care of my visits, even though as a minister there was an allocation for trips on national duties which was equally paltry, so each time I travelled on government work my company had to subsidize the trip. This was the main reason why most MPs were not able to visit their constituencies. I had promised myself to work in government for a short period and thereafter tender my resignation in order to concentrate on developing Chinsali constituency and also run my business.

A Letter of Resignation

I wrote a letter to the President asking for an appointment to see him, but seven months down the line that appointment had still not been granted. The most annoying thing was that every month I had to write a new letter. He was able to grant appointments to so many others, so I felt offended and my nerves were strung up to the last knot. I picked up the phone and called Alexander Chikwanda at State House who was not helpful and asked, "May I know why the President does not want to see me? For the past seven months I have been sending requests through his PR man, Richard Sakala, but I have gotten no answer."

"Maybe because, my sister Katongo, you are difficult and he does not know how to handle you," he replied.

"Surely that is not correct, how can I be difficult to the

owner of the country?" I said.

He told me that the right person to talk to about an appointment with the President was Mr Shimabale, the principal secretary, so I called him saying, "Mr Shimabale as I am talking to you, I am even shaking with anger" (and truly I was). "Tell the President that Katongo says in her capacity she employs people, and when the least employee in her establishment skips over all other bosses and requests to see her she obliges, but here I am, having been asking to meet with the President for the past seven months, and I am not being granted that request. Also tell the President that I never asked for this job. I need to see him."

I was so angry that diplomacy eluded me; I felt unfairly treated.

"Alright Honourable Minister I will get back to you," he said.

An hour later he called and told me the President would see me the next day at 11.00hrs. Later he called to change the time to 16.00hrs.

"Mr Shimabale I am ready even at midnight!" I retorted.

The next day when I went to State House as per appointment, I met Deepak Patel in the lobby who said, "Katongo what is this I hear about your resigning? Please do not, we started this party together and we must see it through together for the sake of our country Zambia."

I told him he was right, but to stay on, one has to be happy and I was not at all happy.

I entered the President's office, found him sitting in a huge chair. We exchanged greetings, then I sat down.

"How can I help you Honourable Minister?" he asked.

"Mr President I brought you this letter, I have resigned with effect from today."

"Honourable Minister may I know the reasons?"

"Mr President I am not happy and my business is suffering."

"How can I help, can I get you an expatriate manager?" he asked.

"No Mr President I am the best manager for my company. I do not need a salary, a car, accommodation or any other incentive, just my presence will turn things round," I said.

"How can I help you financially?"

"Mr President, thank you for the offer, but I always make my money, it may take long but I will always succeed."

"Honourable Minister I do not want you to go because my plans are to elevate you as the first woman Cabinet Minister."

"Thank you for the thought, Mr President. You can give that to Honourable Edith Nawakwi."

It was all quiet, each of us thinking of what next to say. Then he said, "What does my twin brother say about this matter?" He always referred to my husband as his twin brother because it was said they looked alike.

"I am his wife, Mr President, so he supports that which is right for me" I said.

It was all quiet again; as they say: it was so quiet you could hear a pin drop on the carpet!

His last words were: "Honourable Minister I will not read this letter"

It was quiet again and, having exhausted what I had to say, I stood, picked up my ostrich skin handbag and said: "Thank you for your time, Mr President and I hope one day you will open and read the contents of my letter."

I walked out of his office feeling such a relief, that sensational good feeling all over me. A big load had been taken off my shoulder. "I am free," I said to myself, stopped outside the door and did a bit of a *chikokoshi* dance for myself in the State House corridor. From State House I went straight to Cathy Mwanamwambwa's office with an exaggerated clown walk, I entered and announced, throwing my hands in the air: "Hurrah!! You are looking at a free woman!"

"Free from what?" she mused. "Free from the collective responsibilities and the corrupt MMD government. I have just been to see the President and have tendered my letter of resignation, after months of futile attempts to meet with him."

Cathy has been my best friend for close to five decades and she is a friend indeed. I always think that, if I had not met her in New York, my life would have evolved differently. She is kind, generous, loving and above all loyal, and truly nurtures friendship. She brings out the best in whoever she is close to, and that is what has happened to me.

Apart from my company going through problems, I was also going through a lot of soul searching due to what some leaders were alleged to be involved in. I was especially upset by those I thought I knew well, people I had interacted with during the planning for our government, believing that the masses of this country would benefit through our work. When we formed the MMD the majority of members believed the party was poised to run an honest and clean government, that transparency would be of paramount importance and, above all, that we would strive to improve the lives of the citizens. Things turned out to be the exact opposite – all the old vices were surfacing.

At home in the evening I briefed my family that at long last I had met with the President and tendered my resignation. When I mentioned that he had asked how he could help financially, our younger son exploded and asked why I did not accept and ask for K200 million that would do for his school fees? Financially, I was at my lowest ebb; my son could not continue at Drexel University in USA due to non-payment of fees, because as a minister my salary was just K5,350. My answer to him was that accepting Chiluba's money would mean bonding myself even further to this corrupt clique, having automatically to seal my mouth and when he said, "Jump", I'd have to ask "How high must I jump!" I must become his puppet.

"No!" I told my son, "That is not me and not my nature. I love my God-given freedom and I respect myself too much to stoop that low."

The Farewell Meeting with the Electorate of Chinsali Constituency

Soon after I resigned from the government I undertook a trip to the constituency, the purpose was to once more thank the people for the trust and confidence they had in me when they gave me an overwhelming vote over Dr Waza Kaunda, and to tell them that things had not gone the way I expected, and I was not happy being part of this government. Someone stood up and made a passionate plea on behalf of everybody: "Ba Katongo, please don't abandon us and the work you have started, look at the Youth Development Centre you have started, the Women's Business Club you have formed for our wives and mothers. For the first time we can see they are empowered in the true sense. For the men you have helped set up Chinsali Development Company and they are the owners of a Sisu 10-ton truck which is an asset to our community, because it is rendering a great service, transporting agriculture produce for all of us, and the ambulance you have brought for us, so we beg you to rescind the decision."

Another person stood up and said, "Within this short period you have been with us, you have demonstrated that we can see more progress if you stay longer. We have never had such a caring and committed MP."

My answer was, "I appreciate your confidence, and the facts as stated, but you all have gone on record saying MMD leaders are thieves, tell me, are you saying they are thieves with an exception of Katongo Mulenga Maine?"

"No, you are all thieves!" interjected another from the crowd.

I argued that that is one major reason why I should separate myself clearly from the shameless thieves, asking why I should be lumped together with dishonest people when I am not one.

The MMD Government had earned itself a very bad name within a very short time in government, and deservedly so. The corruption and thieving was rampant and blatant. People whose companies were previously tottering were suddenly flourishing. New businesses were being acquired or formed. Money was changing hands under the tables – the shamelessness was just unbelievable.

Some years later, when Chiluba was fighting journalists, *The Post* newspaper in particular, they pulled a fast one on him and exposed the *Zamtrop* account (under Zambia Intelligence) activities. Chiluba used this for his own use, buying obscene quantities of suits and shoes, and to give money to all those he wanted to pacify, just like he wanted to pacify me so that I continue being part of his corrupt government. I found Chiluba to be insincere, a head-knocker, corrupt and above all two-faced. The list of names of beneficiaries of the *Zamtrop* account was long and had some very big names on it, including those from the judiciary. It seemed Chiluba found it hard to draw a line between what belonged to him and what belonged to the state.

Mbita Chitala in 'Not yet Democracy' wrote,

'He actually created a K2 billion slush fund, rubber stamped by Parliament in 1996, and increased it to K4 billion in 1997. In 1996 Chiluba used the slush fund to pay K5 million to each MP for passing the controversial 1996 discriminatory and divisive Constitution, mainly directed at barring Kenneth David Kaunda from contesting any future elections. Corruption also surfaced at Ministry of Education where school desk contracts with many MMD MPs were made and millions were paid from the Treasury for them but the desks were never delivered. Then the *Meridien BIAO Bank (Zambia Limited)* saga where the State "lost" US$87 million was never explained.'

The MMD owed the bank more than K1 billion in an unsecured overdraft obtained under duress which was never serviced. Chitala remembered the party treasurer boasting that, apart from his buying Andrew Sardanis' Chibote Companies, he would also get *Meridien Bank* for nothing.

He wanted to get even with his former boss at *Indeco*, because he felt that Sardanis had once short-changed him in some deal, for which he never forgave him. So, because of a personal vendetta, *Meridien Bank (Zambia Limited)*, a viable enterprise was forced to close and many innocent depositors lost their savings. (Chitala, 2002, pp 102-103)

During Chiluba's tenure of office there was a time when it was alleged Zambia Revenue Authority was instructed to take daily collections to State House, where it ended up in khaki envelopes for distribution. He literally turned State House into a mini Bank of Zambia. The magnitude of the corruption we are seeing today was shamelessly and openly started by the Chiluba regime. Yes, there was corruption in the UNIP government, which was perpetuated by technocrats, but MMD took it to higher levels. The corruption was so blatant that Baldwin Nkumbula and Akashambatwa Mbikusita Lewanika felt uncomfortable in Chiluba's cabinet, and eventually resigned from both the government and the party.

Somehow ordinary members of MMD still found me approachable and would come to me and say that such and such is happening could I please ask 'T' to desist from doing what he is doing. The majority of ordinary members in MMD expected better and different governance from UNIP's, so they were alert, and guarded the party's reputation jealously. On two occasions I had to approach a named person and without even refuting the allegations he asked how, if I did not do the same as he did, I could expect the millions of kwacha I had spent during the campaign to be recovered! I felt chills, goose pimples all over my body.

"But that is not what we discussed when we were planning what to do for the people of Zambia," I reminded him.

"Well, my sister, what is said during the campaign is totally different from actual life thereafter."

I realized how naïve I was in being in league with total strangers, people I thought I knew, but actually knew nothing about. My thinking and theirs were totally opposite; their plans were to enrich themselves in the fastest way possible, while my plans were for development for our people!

It dawned on me what was going on around me and I remembered that my main motive for joining politics had been to get rid of Kaunda and his oppressive government, and help develop Chinsali constituency, but beyond that I had no selfish motive or plans. Others, however, planned to loot the Treasury with impunity. Those whose intentions were to enrich themselves became disgracefully wealthy within a very short time, with no word of caution from the captain of the ship to reprimand any erring minister, because he was playing the same game himself. It was a matter of 'Follow the leader' and it became a free for all. The MMD government was corrupt to the core.

There is no Morality in Politics

Many deputy ministers talked about Chiluba with loathing. One particular MP I was close to would say, "Aunt, I hate the little man" and would describe him with great passion, contempt and anger. I thought it was not healthy to despise someone so much and still work with them.

"Aunt it is different with you, you have something to go back to, while I have nothing, everything I have is from him. If I say 'I am going home', at the end of the house is Chiluba; if I say 'my car', at the end of that car is Chiluba; 'my job' at the end of it is Chiluba. All the same I hate the man."

What a life, I thought to myself. In politics this position is very common, there is no morality only expediency, most people are there to sort out their personal needs, before considering the electorate to whom they promised Heaven on Earth. Most MPs can be considered as needy at the time they enter parliament, thereafter the easy-come money they get as MPs for doing very little corrupts their minds. They become so lazy that they can't think of doing something on their own; they start to avoid trying and just become professional members of parliament for decade after decade. Even when they clearly recognise that the intention or spirit to serve is not in them any more, they shamelessly remain embedded in parliament.

PART SEVEN

My Exit from Politics

Bad Laws that Target Individuals

By 1992, many of us were becoming very uncomfortable with being part of the MMD both as a party and as the government.

In 1993, one parliamentary sitting where we debated the Penal Code left an indelible mark on my mind, and this was the longest sitting we ever had when I was among the legislature. The Speaker did not even allow anybody to drive home for dinner. Instead, he asked all of us to go to the National Assembly Motel for dinner, using parliament buses so that time was observed. Eventually the sitting adjourned at 05.00hrs the following day. I remember Newstead Zimba a tribal cousin quizzing me, *"Iwe kamukazi ka Chibemba,* (You Bemba woman) why do you feel so strongly, about this law, what are you scared of?"

I replied that I was not scared of anything, because I run my life innocently like a small child, but it is people such as him who have issues to worry about, and inadvertently it would rebound on them. I pointed out that the problem with most African legislators is that they are vindictive, short-sighted, and make laws targeting certain individuals who may have diverse thinking from theirs, always about settling scores. They totally forget that they are in a privileged position for just a fraction of their lifetime, and that someday the same bad law they were part of putting in place could be used against them. In my language we say *'Umulandu mume bakumpulafye.'* (A crime is like dew, it clings to you uninvited as you walk).

I for one want to be part of that law which will be good for me, for my children and great-grand-children and the citizenry at large, not one that will be punitive and target a certain group in society. Six months after this law was enacted I was seated in our living room watching the 19.00hrs news bulletin, when there was a report about former MP Petunyala, who in the House was one of the strong supporters of the same law, being picked up, locked up in prison cells, and she cried foul, "This is the law I helped to enact, and now it is being used on me!!"

.   My prophecy became a reality.

In limbo

After I tendered my resignation from the government and while waiting for a reply from the President, I was neither back bencher nor front, so I was not taking part in the deliberations of the House. I sat there; all I could say was 'Hear, hear!' After three months of such nonsense, His Honour the Speaker of the National Assembly, Nabulyato called me to his office and said, "Honourable MP, I do not know what to do or how to handle your case. All I know is the letter to the President which you gave a copy of to me, but the President has not communicated with me over the matter. At the same time I cannot prompt him, we just have to wait until I officially hear from him. As it is, you can't contribute either as front or back bencher, I have been Speaker for many years but have not had such a strange case of resignation"

Meanwhile, a month after I resigned, the President appointed me board chairperson of the Zambia National Service. The letter read: 'In the powers vested in me as President of the Republic of Zambia I appoint you as the Board Chairperson of ZNS by the virtue of you being the Deputy Minister of the Ministry of Youth Sports and Child Development.' I wrote back thanked him and said: 'I will gladly take up the appointment by the virtue of my being Member of Parliament for Chinsali Constituency'. (I know well that ordinary MPs do not qualify for such appointments.) He then asked Hon. Emmanuel Kasonde to talk to me. He said, "My sister, the President has asked me to talk to you that you withdraw the letter of resignation you wrote to him."

"No, I cannot do that because the reasons for which I resigned still stand. Please tell him I say so and that I have considered both sides of the matter very carefully and believe this is the best conclusion."

The week that followed I was summoned by the Republican Vice President to see him during the parliament tea break. His words were, "Hello Katongo, what is this I hear that you have resigned? Why did you not tell me about your intentions? You and me have come a long way. The President has asked me to talk to you to ask you to withdraw the letter of resignation you wrote him."

"Mr Vice President it took me a long time to even get an appointment to see him, seven long months, which is very annoying and demeaning. All the same, if I had told you knowing your situation in this Government, what would you have done about it?"

He reclined in his chair, being the honest and open person he was and said: "You are right, can you imagine I am his Vice, but most times it takes six months without him talking to me in my role as his Vice. We never sit and discuss matters of the country. We just meet at cabinet meetings, and I never know his direct line. By the time I know it, through a third party, it has changed; that is how bad things are."

In parliament amongst back bench MPs I faced a lot of questions such as, "How can you resign from such a prestigious position, most of us wish we were given such an opportunity?"

In my language there is a saying that goes: 'A village you do not live in is admired by its roof tops.' Anyway, I never considered a deputy minister's portfolio as prestigious, given a chance to preside over Zambia for just six months I would do away with that position in most ministries - it is just a waste of taxpayers' money as very few ministries require a deputy. It is a political appeasement position that safeguards the voting power for the sitting government in the House.

Taunted and Nasty Smear Campaign

One day, during the tea break in parliament I got a rude shock when Chilufya Kapwepwe divulged to me the evil gossip that was going around in parliament. It was alleged that a meeting was held in Northern Province by the MPs planning to replace Chiluba with Mr Emmanuel Kasonde as president of the party, as well as for the Republic of Zambia. She asked me whether I had attended this meeting, saying she thought it took place about three months earlier; she had not heard about it at the time and therefore did not attend.

"I am hearing it from you for the first time and did not attend that meeting either," I answered.

"But the rumour goes that you are the one who reported Mr Kasonde to the President because you were there," she told me.

I could not believe my ears and was flabbergasted at the news. I did not think I had enemies in MMD who could fabricate such malicious and unsubstantiated lies about me. In the first place why would I do that against Mr Kasonde? Secondly, I had for many months, to be precise seven months, been trying to no avail to see the President, to hand him the letter of my resignation as deputy minister, so when did I meet him to make that report, I wondered. We went back to the chamber and I sat there trying to find the motive behind this malicious smear, but could not come up with a logical answer.

During the following tea break Dr Rodger Chongwe came to where I was seated and said, "My dear Katongo, what is this I hear that you reported Emmanuel to the President?"

Helplessly I replied, "Rodger I cannot believe the malice, I only learned of it today when Chilufya asked me the same question. I think I will have to ask Hon. Kasonde when he comes back into the country if at all he knows the source."

This was a very sad turn of events for me to be labelled an informer. I hate informers. The fact that I did not know the source of the lies made it even more unbearable.

When Hon. Kasonde returned to the House I went to him during the tea break then posed my question, "I am told there was a meeting amongst MPs from Northern Province which I did not attend. Can you, being the chairman of the Province, tell me when it took place? It is said that during that meeting the subject was to do away with President

Chiluba and replace him with you, and that I reported this to the President. Do you know anything about this?"

He replied that he had first heard of the story when he was in Zimbabwe at our High Commission and that it should not worry me because no such meeting took place. He himself had just brushed it off as one of those political gimmicks to put a wedge between us. No such meeting or plans were being mooted by the Northern MPs and he agreed that this was total malice.

When the President's request that I withdraw my letter of resignation failed, the whole scene turned into smear campaign to malign me. *The Daily Mail* started running fictitious stories that I left the government because I wanted a cabinet position, had reported the Honourable Kasonde to the President and I did not want to work under a fellow woman.

Each time I opened *The Daily Mail* there was something to tarnish my name further. I could only think of State House having a motive to destroy and embarrass me because of not heeding the President's request to withdraw the letter which had somehow made him feel belittled.

I called Richard Sakala, the aide to President Chiluba, and said' "Richard, may I know why you have instructed *The Daily Mail* to fabricate lies about me? I left your corrupt and stinking government, but why taunt me? You tell Chiluba that if the lies do not stop, he will regret it because I for one have absolutely nothing to lose but Chiluba has a lot at stake. Remind him that I say that those living in glass houses should never throw stones."

Of course he denied that he and Chiluba had a hand in all this.

I further called Emmanuel Nyirenda, Editor in Chief of *The Daily Mail.* On hearing my voice he said: "Hallo *Mulamu!*" pretending all was well.

"Don't *'Mulamu'* me," I retorted. "If you were truly my *'mulamu'*, the least you should have done was to talk to me first and not rush into printing lies. I have called you, just to warn you that if you do not desist from writing these malicious lies, I will sue you for every *ngwee* you ever earned in your personal capacity."

Suddenly, all the slurs in the paper stopped, but then I was viciously harassed with yet more instructions from State House that all the business loans I had from various banks be recalled as a way of now completely crippling me financially.

One day I received a call from somebody within the cabinet who alerted me to the instructions from State House to my banks. He felt hurt on my behalf because, as the discussion unfolded, he became aware of the help I rendered to the particular person who was pushing hard for my ruin. It was someone I had helped financially during the 1991 election campaign, a former lecturer at University of Zambia. Each time this man went to Luapula Province for the campaign I would lend him my vanette, with the driver and cash for fuel, and now he was the one who wanted me destroyed.

I confronted him asking, "Do you remember how we met?"

His answer was, "Sis I am at a loss, what do you mean?"

"Of course you should be at a loss, but don't 'sis' me. Just in case you now have conveniently developed amnesia, I will remind you. I had never known, heard of, or met you before MMD, but when you humbly asked for assistance - not even a 'loan' but a 'grant'- I lovingly obliged. Now that you are a cabinet minister, I believe you have forgotten the hurdles you went through and the help you got that made it possible for you to be where you are now. I am now informed that you are the one in the forefront in coming up with ways to finish me off. What kind of a person are you, and what wrong did I do to you? Morally the most you could have done is keep quiet if you found defending me too hard, risky and a threat to your job. I believe what I did for you then was a noble gesture which deserves a noble reward."

Of course he denied being part of the malice. It is certainly true that 'there is no permanent friendship in politics.'

What followed thereafter was a nightmare. One afternoon on my arrival home, the bailiffs had all our furniture and many valuables strewn all over the yard, to be taken for auction. Many fragile and precious items were damaged. I was hurt, but I knew I was paying for resigning from Chiluba's corrupt regime, with absolutely no regrets over my action.

Grain Marketing - A Killer Business

In 1992, I went into maize marketing, a business activity which had previously only been undertaken by the *Food Reserve Agency*, a government funded institution whose main objective was to provide food security to the nation. I must say, of all the businesses I ventured into, this business looked most lucrative on paper, but in reality it had many hidden traps. It was a killer.

The concept was this – the principal had to borrow, against his or her assets (in most cases a building) and enter into a loose agreement with various small scale farmers, who themselves had no collateral to offer as security. The farmer would then receive the fertilizer and seeds (underwritten by the lender) for the coming year's crop and pay back in kind an agreed number of bags of maize for each bag of fertilizer.

When the harvest was due, the principal would provide the empty grain bags for the payment. I remember what happened in my case. On a Friday we provided empty bags and arranged to collect the maize in three days' time. We fuelled our 15-ton truck and hit the road. On arrival there was no maize to collect, because the farmer owed another principal from the previous year that we knew nothing about. According to him, this man just grabbed the crop and left!

That season we could not collect enough to pay back our own loan and because most small scale farmers were not honest, the story kept repeating itself. The next season we believed we had learned, and were wiser by putting various measures in place, but by never reaching 100% collection of what was owed by the farmers, my indebtedness got higher and higher.

It was a very elusive and dangerous business that created a lot of stress, uncertainties and casualties. Some principals just collapsed, and died of heart attack when the property they used as collateral was repossessed by the financial institutions that had extended the loan. Imagine, you have just retired or been retrenched, assume you are making an income generating investment and then the roof over your head is taken away. You are thrown out in the cold – you and your family. In my own case, I lost three properties: a block of flats in Kabwata, a maisonette house in Chainama and a 25-acre plot in Lusaka West. The only consolation was that, on our lawyer's advice, we sold these properties at market value, rather than allowing our assets to be seized – we then paid off the lender from the capital realised.

However, there was one other property that our lender was still holding on to and another one that the Ministry of Lands had dubiously re-entered, the latter not being related to maize marketing. For these two I felt I was a victim while knowing well that the Lord God will not allow one to be punished for doing good. I believe what I did in deciding to share my wealth with the poor farmers was a good gesture on my part, even if they did not honour their obligation but caused me to suffer the consequences. I contacted a practitioner in our Church and asked for prayerful work.

Some months later my lawyer called me and said, "Sissy come and see what I have here."

A letter from the lender's lawyer read: 'Please herein be informed that our client has reviewed your case and taken into consideration the high value of the property staked as collateral. We have decided to find a tenant to take occupation of the warehouse and pay the income to our clients. Once the debt is cleared we will surrender the Title Deed back to you.' My lawyer said, "Sissy this is very strange, I have been in practice for many years but have not previously come across such fair consideration."

I did not divulge to my lawyer that I had requested someone for prayerful work, Divine intervention. I quickly sent an email to my Practitioner in the USA who replied: 'Katongo that is just the beginning, we continue to pray.' On the other property which the Ministry of Lands had re-entered within the same period, someone called me to say, "Mrs Maine, my client wants to buy your property off Lumumba Road."

To which I said that unfortunately it was no longer mine, because the Ministry of Lands took it away from me and gave it to other persons. The man insisted, telling me he did a search and it was all still in my name, and said to be on sale. This was news to me, because four years before, when the ministry re-entered, I had done a search and found a different name. When I went home I explained to my husband who coincidentally had passed by the same place that very morning; it was not in use. He suggested that we should go to the Lands Tribunal.

"No, we can't do that I have committed the case to the Lord," I said and during the night I prayed and asked Him for direction.

The thought came to me that I should write to the Commissioner of Lands and deliver the letter the next day. I wrote: 'Four years ago you re-entered Plot number 1xxx0 and the reasons given were that it was not developed, and yet, the small structure and wall fence were worth quite some millions of kwacha at the time, and now, the person you gave it to is selling, basing the value on what we left. Either you give us back to continue where we left, or compensate us.' The commissioner sent his officer to ascertain my claims. When next I visited his office I was told the paperwork was rectified, and the property was given back to me. I was very grateful to the Almighty God for this great favour.

Concerning the warehouse, six months later my lawyer received yet new correspondence that said, 'Please come and collect the Title Deeds, and also be informed that the balance of K20 million which accrued through interest has been cancelled.' This was unheard of but with Divine intervention anything is possible!

Fortunately, during my heyday in business I used every profit and opportunity I had to invest in land or finished property. I must say, now in my retirement, I survive on rentals from these properties.

Liquidating Kamra

Before I secured an appointment to tender my resignation from the Chiluba government all my personal effects such as potted plants and photos were moved from the ministerial office back to my personal office on Mukatasha Road in the industrial area. As far as I was concerned, politics was now a closed chapter. Another absurd but annoying action was for the housing officer from the Ministry of Supply, to come and demand keys for the alleged government house supposed to be my official residence. You can tell how petty and messy the situation had become. From the beginning I never accepted to move into the government house I had been allocated, and I never even bothered to discover its location because my plans were to resign from the government as soon as possible.

At this point Chiluba had appointed Dr Kabunda Kayongo, a nominated member of parliament as cabinet minister for the Ministry, after Baldwin Nkumbula had resigned citing corruption in the government corridors.

As I said earlier, *Kamra Limited* had been going through a very rough patch, at times not having sufficient materials to finish a line of production. The first thing I administratively handled was to lay off some workers because the salary bill was hefty. The importation of raw materials from Italy became sporadic, meaning that turnover had been drastically affected. I had to swallow a bitter pill and go into voluntary liquidation. I sold the machinery to enable me to pay off the bank overdraft instead of waiting to be declared bankrupt, which would have complicated all my future business endeavours. The only fortunate part was I still had assets to fall back on, but all the same it was painful to see *Kamra* go under.

The National Party is Formed

Prior to my resignation from the MMD the majority of us were openly not welcomed, in short we were being hounded out of the party. At the same time the corrupt activities that were going on were choking us, so we strongly felt we must move on.

After we resigned from MMD, twelve of us decided, in 1993, to form a new party and named it the National Party. Dr Inonge Mbikusita-Lewanika was the Interim Chairperson/Caretaker. We agreed to go for a convention. Most of us had not yet recovered from the financial bashing of the MMD campaign and could not contribute much to the convention budget. The contenders for presidency of the new party were: Hon. Kasonde, Hon. Nkumbula, Hon. Dr Inonge Mbikusita-Lewanika, and Hon. Humphrey Mulemba. Of the four, Hon. Kasonde was seemingly the strongest candidate, but like all of us he was low on resources.

Hon. Nkumbula felt that since he was single-handedly funding the convention he would call the shots about the venue and other logistics to his own benefit. The night before we travelled to Monze where the convention was to take place we had a short meeting at Hon. Kasonde's house, just the three of us. I appealed to Hon. Nkumbula that he give a chance to Hon. Kasonde, but he kept quiet, implying, 'What are you talking about, am I not good enough?'

I then said to him, "You are taking us to Monze, your home area, which will disadvantage the other candidates. I can foresee a situation where the National Party is buried in Monze because the elections will not be free and fair."

And indeed, when the convention took place it was sad to observe the behaviour of his supporters, especially those who were in charge of catering. They would loudly announce,

151

"Food is available only for Nkumbula's supporters."

Supporters had come from as far as Northern, Western and North Western Provinces, hungry and tired, just to be told there was no food for them. The Tongas were in charge and tribalism was showing its ugly teeth! We ended up feeding our supporters individually from the restaurants on the streets of Monze. The elections were conducted and Hon. Nkumbula won the presidency of National Party. After the announcement of the election results I walked out of the room to get some fresh air outside. Two Nkumbula supporters were going through an election post-mortem, the young lady said, "Hey, did you hear Mr Kasonde's presidential speech. He was just terrific, and very articulate, If only he was not Bemba I would have given him my vote."

Her partner answered, "Me too."

I joined in the conversation and said, "For now, you guys can celebrate as much as you want but one thing you should know and bear in mind is that there is no National Party because of tribalism. The party is dead and buried right here in Monze."

In the evening after the elections I addressed my supporters, who had come all the way from Northern Province, saying, "Thank you very much for the trust, confidence, and support you have shown and given me this far, but I must say this is the end of my political journey and involvement in politics because National Party is dead and buried right here in Monze."

My conviction was, and still is, that morality has no place in politics.

Election as National Party Candidate

In 1993, after the National Party was formed it was in a quandary as to who would stand on the National Party ticket in Chinsali constituency because the resources and time to put up a formidable campaign were too short. Despite my earlier decision to exit politics, I was forced to stand as no other candidate came up from National Party. I was supported by Mr Emmanuel Kasonde and Dr

Inonge Mbikusita-Lewanika, while Baldwin Nkumbula and Akashambatwa Lewanika (though National party members) supported Chilufya Kapwepwe, an independent candidate. Their perverse action allowed the Chinsali people to judge National Party harshly. The unity in National Party was not there; even siblings were not working together. When this happened, I concluded finally and finally that National Party would not be any different from MMD and that my political exit must be now and not later!

Things Fall Apart

My world fell apart when Abe, my beloved husband, suddenly passed on in March 2002. He got sick on a Tuesday, and on Friday he was no more. All the thirty three years we were together he never was sick, not a single day, except for once with a toothache.

He was a very loving and down-to-earth person who was liked by many people and the activities during his funeral also confirmed this fact. I did not spend a cent on this; all the food, transport, videos and the expensive casket were given by friends, neighbours and acquaintances and, despite the funeral period being longer than normal, there was more than enough food throughout. My heartfelt gratitude still goes to all those who contributed to making my burden lighter.

Abe had become my best friend and companion as well as my husband, and he was an awesome dad to our two sons. Two months before his passing on we had concluded that, come June 2002, we would spend some time in South Africa and establish where our new home would be. As usual, he lovingly asked my preference. 'Cape Town' was my prompt answer. I had visited Cape Town on many occasions, each time the feeling was the same, that it was the place where I would like to spend my retirement, of course in the company of Abe.

My coping mechanism when he passed on was to occupy every minute of my time so that I would have none to give me chance to brood over my sudden loss. Because the pain and the state of hopelessness was unbearable, I buried myself in *The Bible* and *Science and Health with Key to the Scripture* by Mary Baker Eddy. My great Divine Comforter answered me and was always there and continues to be there for me.

With Abe's passing on all plans went into disarray and I must say that in haste I made a lot of financial mistakes, such as selling White Rose Farm, believing migrating to South Africa would lessen the pain because I would be with our two sons there. I continued praying and asking for Divine guidance. As time went on I realized it would after all not be a wise move, concluding that at my age it would be very difficult to adjust and make new friends in a new place. Here, at home in Zambia I had relatives, friends and familiar culture.

Special memories continue to linger on. I remember one morning I was awake in bed but lay there waiting for my usual morning cup of steaming lemon tea to be served by my beloved husband who spoilt me and did that for many years. The thought came, 'There is no tea coming ever again because Abe is no more.' I sadly had to get up and make myself that cup of tea.

To add to my grief, seven months later, our first son Ralesite passed on in South Africa where he resided. The feeling of the loss of a youthful life, a child whom you carried for nine months, is beyond description. The feeling was choking and for many years that followed I would sometimes stop in my tracks and ask myself: 'Katongo, who are you grieving for, your husband, or your son?' Our son, Ralesite always had a big loving heart for his mother and the family at large. He was one of the youngest of his cousins from my siblings, Lebby and Dorothy. He saw me regularly clean the surrounding of our Dad's grave. He took over and said, "Mum I will organize my big cousins, and we grandchildren will from now on keep Grandfather's grave clean."

That was done for many years until he relocated to South Africa and there was no more cleaning of Grandpa's grave.

The caring son he was, one time he called as routine to check on his mum. Over the phone he picked up the fact that I was low in spirit.

"Mum, are you alright?" he inquired.

"Son, I am fine, it is just that I have disembarked from the minibus and in this October heat I feel exhausted."

"You are on public transport? What about your double-cab?"

I explained to him that the engine was giving problems but his Dad and Mum were now tired out and had given up struggling with this sort of thing.

"Mum I am on my way to Durban on business, I will buy the 2.5L engine you need and send it to you. I will use some of my savings for the down payment on the house I intend to buy knowing well that if there is a shortfall I can get help from you later."

He sent not only the engine to make us mobile but also a minibus that I wanted to generate daily income.

I was very happy to receive the minibus, however, my son was not so sure and warned me that the minibus business could be a thorn in my flesh because most drivers in this sector were very undisciplined, not very honest and, therefore, difficult to control. I did not heed the advice given to me because I somehow thought I would manage, after all I had run many businesses successfully. Within six months I had employed three different drivers, the bus was in a deplorable condition, with tattered seats and the climax came when the windscreen was shattered. I asked the driver who was to repair it and casually he stated that the 'insurance would pay'. His casualness made me so angry and that was the end of me and the minibus business. On the surface the business seems lucrative but the truth is that the driver who never invests a penny is the major beneficiary. I repaired the bus and sold it.

Ten days after Abe passed on, my mother, who lived with us, passed on in the same house. Six months later my favourite younger sister, Beatrice who also lived with me passed on and I was left alone in our big farm house. 2002 was the darkest year in my life! I fell apart and it took a long while to pull myself together.

Virtually a Zombie

When Katyala, our second son who lives in SA came to visit me around three years after the passing on of my husband he realized his mother was not the same strong and decisive person she had always been. He pleaded with me to buy myself a safer vehicle, because the old double-cab I'd been driving for years had seen better days. He said it worried him so much that whenever he got a call from me he immediately thought I must have had a breakdown.

He was right, the double-cab was a mess, but more importantly, so was I. Being a member of Lions Clubs International, after every meeting I would look around in the Lion's Den with no shame and ask my fellow Lion members to come and push-start my jalopy and I am sure it was out of sympathy that they pushed. When I look back I see that definitely it was not me in my normal senses.

When I told my son I had no money to buy a new car he protested, "Mum, don't forget, you are talking to your own son. The money is not the issue here. The point is that your safety is at stake."

He realized his message did not sink in, so he decided to pester me morning, noon and night – eventually I saw sense and reluctantly sent someone to SA who bought me a nice little car, a Toyota Corsa and when I drove around Lusaka, I got comments like, 'That is a nice car' and for sure it was. At the same time I was enjoying the complements, the comfort and the style of it. I was beginning to be myself again. When my son returned to SA I realised I owed him a thank you for opening my eyes as well as clearing my psychological block, I called him and thanked him from deep down in my heart.

I turned round the whole episode and asked myself the question: 'What else do I need to change?' I realized I had been going in circles and it took my son to come all the way from South Africa to awaken me. I had virtually become a zombie.

In 2008, I became an Independent Herbalife Distributor for a networking company whose nutritional products were just fantastic. The first thing that I did was to lose a bit of the excess fat that had built up around me. I quickly became a Supervisor, then a World Team presenter. Herbalife was fairly new on the Zambian market, having been reintroduced by Andrea Limbredes who came from Cyprus. I became very committed to the cause of making Zambia a healthy nation through these nutritional products, as well as changing peoples' lives while earning an income. Trips to the Copperbelt, namely Ndola, Kitwe and Chingola, were frequent, organised by Andrea who co-opted me in her Team as second presenter. Instead of just changing other peoples' lives, my own also changed in the process. I was busy, energised, happy and created a steady income for myself. My world changed for the best. With Herbalife I travelled to Barcelona for Extravaganza, Sun City, Cape Town, Durban and Johannesburg for Extravaganza and Regional Leadership meetings. This suits me well because I love travelling.

In 2012, my son Katyala got married to Nonzwakazi, a wonderful daughter I never had. They made me whole as the grandmother of two beautiful little creatures, Ralesite and Katongo. Thanks to the technology I am able to talk to my beloved little friends on a videocall ever so often. They live and work in Johannesburg, South Africa, Katyala as a business man while Nonzwakazi is an accountant.

In 2016, I embarked on a pine timber plantation in Muchinga Province, which I have named 'Ralekatoo Timber Plantation' after my two beloved and precious grandchildren. At my age of 74 I am busy and enjoying the work of planting trees as one way of contributing to a clean environment of our planet.

Afterword

I have made several references to Honourable Mbita Chitala's book *Not yet Democracy* because it impacted on me heavily as being factual and well researched. He was part of the inner circle and therefore had first-hand information. When I went to his house to collect his book, I remember his being apologetic about the fact that the book reflected so much anger, but I agree with him that being part of MMD just made you feel angry, especially, for those of us not involved in corrupt dealings. It was shameful and not what we had expected the new party to turn out to be.

When Honourable Levy Mwanawasa resigned as Vice President of MMD and the government, I went to his law firm office and said, "Levy, I just came to congratulate you for the move which has been long overdue."

"I tell you it has not been easy for me when they do unethical things behind my back and expect me to face and explain to the nation, no, I am tired I cannot continue, all in the name of collective responsibility." He said this with so much choking anger.

Those who are rigid, principled and set in their dealings will find no joy nor satisfaction in politics because what matters is not what should be or what ought to be or what one believes in, but the mob psychology euphemistically, referred to as "collective responsibility."

I clearly remember our late cousin, Martin Luo, trying to save me from the imminent heartaches he foresaw for me once I joined politics. His words were, "My sister, I know very well that you do not carry a fibre of a politician in you. As a journalist I have worked with so many politicians who I believe do not know the difference between TRUTH and UNTRUTH, HONESTY and DISHONESTY. I am not sure you will fit in as a politician."

I was very annoyed with him because I felt he was underestimating me.

In summary all I am saying is politics is not carved out for everyone. When I was in the deep waters of politics I began to see what my cousin earlier referred to as not knowing the difference between the TRUTH and the UNTRUTH, or HONESTY and DISHONESTY.

Most politicians are void of principles and are able to sell their souls for short term benefits, which in the first place is their main attraction to politics. As for women in politics, to succeed one does not have to be reckless like the one time Eastern Province female MP and sell your soul to the highest bidder, jumping from one political party to another, all the time looking for material gain without qualms or shame. But, decent women when they enter the political arena will take a low profile because, somehow the 'collective responsibility' keeps nibbling at their conscience.

Also, in my opinion, as a female MP you represent a family, while a male MP represents just himself as an individual. I must say most women are more humane and sensitive to issues than the menfolk. One thing about politics is there are just too many other things one is not in control of – to be successful you do not have to be jelly-like or follow the wind but must genuinely be yourself. If you are a woman of integrity and considerate you will earn the respect you deserve.

Business and Politics

I, for one, found it very difficult to run a successful business whilst serving as a full-time politician because for me 'full-time' meant just that. Most of us from the business community failed lamentably, because the business took second or third position in importance. The other major reason is that most Zambian companies are a 'one man show', the structures may be there but the CEO makes all big and minor decisions. If he/she is absent for just a month the impact is felt, so much more so if absent for five years, the full parliamentary session!

THE END

Acknowledgments

Writing a book appears to be an individual project, but the reality is that it takes an entire team to come up with a product that thousands or even millions will read and appreciate. I would like to acknowledge most humbly and sincerely the kind and encouraging comments from friends and relatives who read the book while in draft form. My deepest, gratitude to Nigel Watt, an author and publisher for the first edit of the book. He happened to be on a short holiday in Zambia when Rosemary Mumbi asked me if it was in order for Nigel to go through the book. Nigel you came in just at the right time and helped me put the pieces together and we end up with a masterpiece.

I thank my niece, Musonda Kaluba for the valuable contribution in shaping this book, at times reminding me of some forgotten details.

I am deeply grateful to Albert Mulenga Mumba, my primary school classmate for his contribution especially on the happenings during our primary school days. I can never ask for a better critique. After reading the manuscript, he actually helped me understand my own thoughts even better.

My sister, Dorothy and my brother-in-law, Ephraim Kaluba I am indebted to you for being there for me at many a point. In your sweet humble spirits you have guided and moulded me in a very special way. You know very well that without the two of you I would not be the person I am today or be able to even write this book. Dorothy, I love the way you play the mother-hen act around all of us, your siblings and the whole family at large.

Katyala, my son and my daughter-in-law, Nonzwakazi thank you very much for giving me the most handsome grandson, Ralesite and the most beautiful granddaughter, Katongo. I love and cherish them dearly.

My heartfelt gratitude goes to Mary Masase, who has tirelessly given guidance and direction to the book.

My gratitude goes to my grandson, Ernest Mubanga Kabumbu the IT geek. For me a computer is a complicated device but for him, his answer is always a cool, 'No problem'. Without him I would still be making statements like. "AM GOING TO WRITE A BOOK, but when?"

I would be failing if I do not thank Mr Kaule Siulapwa, for the valuable guidance he gave me, being the first person I gave the very raw manuscript to.

My heartfelt gratitude goes to Pamela Shurmer-Smith for being a fantastic editor thereby improving and heightening the quality of the book which I know was not easy working with a first time author.

Printed in the United States
By Bookmasters